How to Reach the Hard to Teach

ASCD
ALEXANDRIA, VIRGINIA USA

How to Reach the Hard to Teach

Excellent
Instruction
for Those Who
Need It Most

JANA
ECHEVARRÍA

NANCY
FREY

DOUGLAS
FISHER

1703 N. Beauregard St. • Alexandria, VA 22311-1714 USA
Phone: 800-933-2723 or 703-578-9600 • Fax: 703-575-5400
Website: www.ascd.org • E-mail: member@ascd.org
Author guidelines: www.ascd.org/write

Deborah S. Delisle, *Executive Director*; Robert D. Clouse, *Managing Director, Digital Content & Publications*; Stefani Roth, *Publisher*; Genny Ostertag, *Director, Content Acquisitions*; Julie Houtz, *Director, Book Editing & Production*; Katie Martin, *Editor*; Melissa Johnston, *Graphic Designer*; Mike Kalyan, *Manager, Production Services*; Barton Matheson Willse & Worthington, *Typesetter*; Kelly Marshall, *Senior Production Specialist*

All web links in this book are correct as of the publication date below but may have become inactive or otherwise modified since that time. If you notice a deactivated or changed link, please e-mail books@ascd.org with the words "Link Update" in the subject line. In your message, please specify the web link, the book title, and the page number on which the link appears.

PAPERBACK ISBN: 978-1-4166-2238-3   ASCD product #116010   n8/16
PDF E-BOOK ISBN: 978-1-4166- 2240-6; see Books in Print for other formats.
Quantity discounts: 10–49, 10%; 50+, 15%; 1,000+, special discounts (e-mail programteam @ascd.org or call 800-933-2723, ext. 5773, or 703-575-5773). For desk copies, go to www.ascd.org/deskcopy.

Library of Congress Cataloging-in-Publication Data

Names: Echevarría, Jana, 1956- author. | Frey, Nancy, 1959- author. |
    Fisher, Douglas, 1965- author.
Title: How to reach the hard to teach : excellent instruction for those who need it most /
    Jana Echevarría, Nancy Frey, Douglas Fisher.
Description: Alexandria, Virginia, USA : ASCD, [2016] | Includes bibliographical references
    and index.
Identifiers: LCCN 2016021748 (print) | LCCN 2016030899 (ebook) |
    ISBN 9781416622383 (pbk.) | ISBN 9781416622406 (PDF)
Subjects: LCSH: Children with social disabilities—Education—United States.
    | Slow learning children–United States. | Linguistic minorities–Education—
    United States.
Classification: LCC LC4091 .E27 2016 (print) | LCC LC4091 (ebook) | DDC 371.826/94–dc23
LC record available at https://lccn.loc.gov/2016021748

24 23 22 21 20 19 18 17 16   1 2 3 4 5 6 7 8 9 10 11 12

How to Reach the Hard to Teach

Excellent Instruction for Those Who Need It Most

1. Every Child Achieves When
   There Is an Opportunity to Learn 1

2. The Expectation of Success 18

3. Access to the Core Curriculum 38

4. Assessment to Inform Instruction 68

5. Language Instruction 103

6. A Supportive Climate and Culture 134

Conclusion 158

References 160

Index 166

About the Authors 173

Every Child Achieves When There Is an Opportunity to Learn

Rita Elwardi's high school English students participated in an interdisciplinary unit organized around an essential question: *Why do people move?* The unit's focus was migration and immigration. It featured several informational texts and a literary one (a novel) and incorporated content related to geography, economics, and climate studies.

On the first day of the unit, after introducing the essential question and the purpose for the day, Ms. Elwardi announced the opening activity—a quick-write that would tap into students' background knowledge and prior experiences. She asked her students to write for 10 minutes about a moment when they had to say good-bye.

Ms. Elwardi's students are a diverse group. Many of them speak a language other than English at home. A majority live in poverty and have a history of struggling in school. Although they attend school in a busy urban center a few miles from a prosperous downtown, in terms of their present lives, the region's economic possibilities might as well be thousands of miles away. Student mobility is high, the result of families moving frequently in search of better lives for their children. Almost every student enrolled in Ms. Elwardi's English language arts classes has attended many schools and lived in many different neighborhoods. Saying good-bye has become a routine part of their young lives.

While the class began the quick-write, Ms. Elwardi walked about the room and spoke privately with students not yet putting pencil to paper. With each, she followed a process designed to get them started, asking prompting questions (see Figure 1.1) and taking notes as they replied. "That's just what I'm looking for, Horacio," she assured one boy. "Write what you just told me, and continue writing down your thoughts, one after another, from that point on until the memory is complete."

Circling the room again, Ms. Elwardi scanned the responses of students who had stopped writing and asked them clarifying questions to prompt further exploration. Here is one student's response, with the irregularities in grammar and punctuation preserved:

> On November 15, 1996, it was winter and too cold. At that time I was so sad because I was coming to America. I think I couldn't see anymore my country, my cousins and relatives, my country's church, also my mother. One word was hard to say for my mother. It was Good-bye. Because I never left my mother for a long time or even a few days before I came to United States. My feeling was bad like a sad for two weeks before I came to USA. I was counting each day and I thought how do I say good-bye for my mother, cousins, relatives and my country? I was looking all around and I was crying.
>
> At last the day, November 15, 1996, came. But at that time I was not sad and I was well. I thought, "Now I can to say good-bye for my mother," and I told to myself. Each minute and hour were decreasing. I was ready and I went to my mother and I hugged. I was looking at the ground and I couldn't say good-bye. Both of us were crying. I remember that time. I never forget I couldn't say good-bye.

FIGURE 1.1
Guiding Questions That Elicit Details

- Where and when did this take place?
- Who was with you, and why?
- Why did you have to leave this place or say good-bye to this person?
- What did you say, and what did the others say to you?
- What were you thinking before, during, and after this moment?
- How do you feel now that you are looking back at the moment?

With the quick-writes completed, the class went on to a collaborative oral language-building activity called the Three Step Interview (Kagan, 1994), which encourages active listening. Grouped into fours (Students A, B, C, D) and partnered within their group (A with B, C with D), the students read their quick-writes aloud, telling their own stories. Then they retold the stories their partners had shared. Afterward, the students revised their quick-writes to improve clarity, to make them more vivid, and to be sure the writing captured the memory's key information and feelings.

Next up was a writing activity called Found Poetry (Dunning & Stafford, 1992). Ms. Elwardi used her own quick-write as a model, posting it on a document camera. She explained the procedure to the class: "As I read my quick-write, I'll underline the important words and phrases that convey sensory details and express the tone of my writing. Then I'll take those words and phrases and restructure them into an open-verse poem."

As Ms. Elwardi walked through the classroom, giving individual assistance and encouragement, her students "found the poetry" in the quick-writes they'd written and then revised. Here is the found poem in the quick-write we shared earlier:

Winter
too cold, so sad,
coming to America.

one word was hard to say—
Good-bye.
How do I say it
to my mother,
cousins, relatives,
and my country?
I was counting,
the last day came.
I was counting
each hour, each minute
decreasing.
Looking at the ground,
crying,
I hugged my mother.
I remember that time,
I couldn't say
Good-bye.

There are several reasons we wanted to tell this story. The first is an obvious one: Rita Elwardi is an amazing teacher, one of the finest we have ever known. Her professional practice embodies every one of the principles we explore in this book. She sets high expectations of success, provides access to the core curriculum, monitors her students' progress and provides necessary supports, attends to language development, and creates a supportive classroom climate. In the slice of classroom life we showed, Ms. Elwardi used a series of writing exercises to introduce her students to a novel they were about to read. In the unit's culminating project, they went on to answer the unit's essential question—*Why do people move?*—in writing, using evidence from several texts, including the novel. Her objective was for students to respond in ways that honored their personal experiences but also looked beyond the personal to analyze the perspectives presented in the various texts. For Ms. Elwardi, inviting students to write about their experience was a means of providing them access to the core curriculum.

The second reason we told this story has to do with the student writer, whom we'll call Renata. She arrived in the United States at age 11, having been transported by human smugglers who had charged her mother an exorbitant amount of money to do so. Renata's mother was desperate to protect her youngest daughter from the crime that had spread through their rural village, a side effect of a thriving illegal drug trade. In the United States, Renata was cared for by an older sister; after a few months, the sister's new boyfriend insisted that Renata move out of the house and into a moving box in the backyard, and that is what she did.

When Renata joined Ms. Elwardi's class, she was a largely silent girl who often disappeared into the background. But Ms. Elwardi saw a quick mind. Over the course of the year, Ms. Elwardi focused on helping Renata learn about herself, the world, and its possibilities. Through the advocacy of her teacher and the help of many others, Renata moved to a safe home, transferred to honors courses, and graduated from high school. Because she had the good fortune to live in a state where undocumented people are able to attend the university, Renata graduated from college and went on to earn an advanced degree in social work. Working through the legal system, she was able to obtain U.S. citizenship. Today Renata works for a nonprofit that specializes in advocating for young Latinas.

Of course we would never say that Renata's success is due entirely to one lesson that one teacher taught. But Renata has told us that on that day, Ms. Elwardi sparked in her a level of self-awareness that she hadn't experienced before. In turn, after reading Renata's quick-write and the poetry it contained, Ms. Elwardi looked at Renata in a different way. All teachers have had this experience—that moment when we see children in a new light and realize all they might achieve. This book is about shining that light on those who are too often overlooked. It's about taking action to change the lives of the students typically considered the hardest to reach and, therefore, the hardest to teach.

Reaching the Hardest to Teach

The "hardest-to-teach" children who sit in our classrooms can make themselves known in obvious ways, chiefly by failing to make expected progress on academic measures. Some of these students have formal paperwork (e.g., an Individualized Education Program [IEP] or a 504 plan) that identifies their specialized learning needs and articulates a plan for them to gain access to the core curriculum; others do not. Some of these students are growing up in English-speaking households; many others are not.

This is where our look at the students who are traditionally thought of as the hardest to teach begins: with students who have disabilities and with students who are learning English. Until recent times, both were customarily served in separate classrooms or facilities, clustered with similarly labeled children. This approach was thought to be necessary in order to provide these students with access to the core curriculum, which is a foundational principle in public education. Because the needs of these students weren't widely understood, it was thought that only a relatively small portion of the teaching force, armed with specialized training, could teach them.

However, as society's perspectives have shifted, so have teacher education and placement practices. Both social justice issues and a growing body of evidence about best practices have converged. While there is still much to be improved, special education literature now emphasizes the general educator's content knowledge, collaboration skills, and provision of access to the core curriculum as vital factors for student success (Villa, Thousand, & Nevin, 2013). These perspectives run parallel to current best practices for helping English learners access the core curriculum. We are not saying that learning a new language is a disability; it's a gift. However, like students with identified disabilities, English learners need skilled teachers who know how to provide them access to the general curriculum.

Today, children identified as English learners are found in classrooms all over the United States, not just in regions historically associated with migration. Nancy, who has spent her teaching career in Florida and California (two places with significant English learner populations), once found herself eating lunch at a conference held in a small city of 40,000 less than one hour's drive from the Canadian border. She was joined by two local English as a second language (ESL) specialists who supported nearly 100 children at 4 area elementary schools. Collectively, these students spoke 38 different languages and had widely varied educational histories. Some were the children of university professors or oil and gas exploration executives, while others had interrupted schooling experiences because of war and violence in their countries of origin.

According to these ESL specialists, they operated in a system with outdated models of support for English learners that shortchanged children and marginalized teachers. As itinerant educators, they spent just a few hours a week with their students, mostly providing pullout supports such as phonics and vocabulary instruction, or in some cases, content teaching. It simply wasn't enough time. "I can't keep doing this," one said. "What I'm doing isn't working for my kids, their teachers, or me." When asked to elaborate, they cited having no time to work with classroom teachers on aligning instruction. "The [classroom] teachers would like to know how to support these kids better, but they say they don't have the training," said one. "Over time the English learners in their classes become 'my kids' instead of theirs. They hoped that the ESL specialist could address all of the needs, but it really will take us all." As we discuss specifically in Chapter 5, *all* teachers must be language teachers, given that English learners are present in nearly every school in the United States and given the increased language demands that today's academic standards place on all students.

Who else falls into the "hardest-to-teach" population? We also include the students who fly under the radar, undetected until an astute teacher spots them. We are talking about students like Renata, whose genius has been muted by difficult circumstances in addition to a new language. We're talking about the boy who makes jokes all the time—not to "get attention" but to distract you from noticing he doesn't understand the task. The girl who shrinks in her seat when you glance her way, not out of shyness but because she is hoping you won't call on her for an answer she can't supply. The child who repeatedly brings you small gifts from home because her dad is hoping you'll regard his daughter kindly when she struggles to follow directions. The category includes all the students who do not have an identified disability and who are not learning English but, for a variety of reasons we may or may not grasp, underachieve. Perhaps they were slow to learn how to read. Perhaps chronic absenteeism in the primary grades, defined as 10 days or more in a school year, negatively affected their reading proficiency, grit, and perseverance (Ginsburg, Jordan, & Chang, 2014). Whatever the cause, these students have been unable to find themselves academically. Over time, they begin to engage in destructive self-talk that moves from "I don't get this" to "I'm stupid," and from "This is stupid" to "I don't care."

What all children who underperform need, whether they have formal paperwork or not, is a clear path forward—an on-ramp to the learning highway. Constructing that ramp requires intentionality. In other words, our struggling students cannot be overlooked, and they cannot be an afterthought. It is not sufficient to design instruction for most, and then retrofit it for the few who are on the learning fringes. Nor is it enough to hope that geography and good luck bring the students who most need help into the classrooms of teachers who are equipped to help them. All of us need to *be* those teachers, and that requires us to take explicit action.

The Way Forward: The Five Essential Practices of Excellent Instruction

There is ample evidence that specific practices improve the outcomes for students who do not have a history of academic success. The simple fact that students who fail in one school will achieve in another provides additional reason to hope that a different approach can be the difference (e.g., Ross, McDonald, Alberg, & McSparrin-Gallagher, 2007).

Our collective research, professional experiences in effective schools, and own teaching careers suggest that increasing the likelihood of every student's success is a matter of adhering to five principles of excellent instruction. Doing so is absolutely essential if we hope to bring out the hidden genius in our underachieving students.

1. **Provide access to the core curriculum.** Students who are learning English, struggling, or otherwise falling short of their potential don't need watered-down, "dumbed-down," curriculum. They don't need isolated skills practice. A 6th grader who is taught 3rd grade standards will likely be performing as a strong 4th grader in 7th grade. What these students need are teachers who know how to remove or otherwise circumvent barriers to the core curriculum, and know how to support students' development and accelerate their growth. This requires differentiated instruction and scaffolded learning. Without access to quality curriculum, students will stagnate, falling further and further behind; with access, they have the chance to explore complex ideas, think critically, and apply their learning creatively. Access is foundational, but access alone isn't enough.

2. **Establish a climate that supports students as individuals and learners.** Every student enters the classroom with his or her background knowledge, lived experiences, values,

beliefs, traditions, and ideas. These understandings factor into the learning experience, and they must be honored as scaffolds that will support new knowledge and understanding. A classroom learning environment that feels safe enough to encourage risk taking is especially critical for students with a history of academic struggle. For them, trying might very well mean failing (at first), and they must believe that their efforts won't be mocked or belittled, and that if they keep trying (and accept feedback), they will eventually succeed. It's the experience of learning that builds students' identity as learners. Students who find school difficult must have teachers who are both culturally sensitive and culturally proficient—willing to look beyond themselves and their own experiences to create a learning community that honors individuals and celebrates differences.

3. **Set high expectations for success.** Study after study has demonstrated that teacher belief in students' capacity to achieve has a significant impact on actual student achievement. Students rise to the expectations their teachers set. All students must understand what they are expected to learn and why they should learn it. They need high expectations for academic language, critical thinking, and engagement. It's essential that struggling students have teachers who acknowledge and support the aspirations they have for themselves. They need learning experiences that open their eyes to the vast array of possibilities that lie before them and present pathways to achieve short- and long-term goals. And, critically, there must be responsive systems in place that teachers can readily activate when students fall short of high expectations.

4. **Provide language instruction.** Humans learn through language. When we interact with others, through speaking, listening, reading, writing, and viewing, we acquire new

insights, skills, and experiences. Language should permeate the classroom, and students who struggle in school should receive explicit instruction in language. Some need specific, dedicated time for English language instruction, and all need access to the academic language that will open the doors to classroom learning and facilitate their membership in the literate community.

5. **Provide assessment-informed instruction.** Struggling students need teachers who know how to uncover what they already know and can measure their evolving skills and understanding, stay abreast of their shifting needs, and take regular, informed action to keep their learning on track toward the identified goals. It's critical that their teachers know and employ formative assessment techniques.

Together, these principles have the power to radically change lives, and not just the lives of students. When teachers use these five principles, they feel more successful. They become empowered professionals who apply sound pedagogical know-how to make informed decisions that impact students' learning.

The principles of excellent instruction outlined in this book draw on and extend our previous works: the Framework for Intentional and Targeted Teaching® (FIT Teaching®) and the Sheltered Instructional Observation Protocol (SIOP®). The FIT Teaching approach, created by Doug and Nancy, unifies nearly two decades of work on educational excellence to clarify the most effective planning, instruction, and assessment practices (Fisher, Frey, & Arzonetti Hite, 2016). SIOP, co-developed by Jana and colleagues (Echevarría, Vogt, & Short, 2000, 2017), is a widely used model of instruction for English learners empirically shown to improve their access to the curriculum and raise their achievement (Short, Echevarría, & Richards-Tutor, 2011).

Learning is a complex process, and facilitating it requires teachers to apply pedagogical content knowledge—first to build student knowledge and then to deepen it. Within FIT Teaching, this staged approach is called Instructing with Intention. It means providing

- *Focused instruction* that clearly communicates the purposes for learning and the measures of success, and uses modeling and think-alouds to explicitly demonstrate how experts understand the content
- *Guided instruction* that gradually releases responsibility to the learner; provides questions, prompts, and cues to scaffold learning; and takes note of when learning has stalled
- Opportunities for *collaborative learning* where students use academic language in the company of their peers to resolve problems, propose solutions, and create products
- Opportunities for *independent learning* where students deepen and extend their understanding through spiral review, application, and opportunities to self-regulate

The SIOP Model has similar components that reflect excellent instruction, but it also includes features that are critical for English learners, such as adapting content to students' English proficiency levels and using visuals and other techniques to make the content understandable.

FIT Teaching and SIOP intersect with our five targeted principles in a number of ways, including the expectations we hold for students and the academic and linguistic supports we use to help them move through a learning progression and develop their capacity to meet the transfer goals necessary for meaningful learning. Finally, in line with our belief that what happens in a school's hallways and common spaces seeps into its classrooms, our approach also incorporates aspects of FIT Teaching's Cultivating a Learning Climate component, which focuses on solidifying students' confidence that their teachers and the school administrators see every student's potential and will do everything to nurture it.

Ensuring the Opportunity to Learn

Despite the media claims to the contrary, a majority of students in most U.S. schools do well (e.g., Berliner & Biddle, 1996). But *most* students isn't *all* students. It certainly doesn't include students who don't read well, many who are learning English, and many who live in poverty.

A growing body of evidence drawn from large-scale national and international data suggests that every school includes some students who have fewer opportunities to learn than their classmates (Schmidt, Burroughts, Zoido, & Houang, 2015). It is worth noting that *opportunity to learn* (OTL) requires exposure to rigorous and challenging content. Children who live in poverty, English language learners, and students with disabilities are especially vulnerable to restricted OTL, which can also be attributed to organizational practices and policy decisions. Schmidt and colleagues go on to explicitly state that the "systematically weaker content offered to lower-income students" has a negative effect. "Rather than ameliorating educational inequalities, schools were exacerbating them" (p. 380). In other words, the unintended effect of watering down the curriculum, slowing the pace, and tracking students into remedial course work magnifies, rather than reduces, knowledge gaps. These gaps become more difficult to overcome with each year of a student's schooling.

Yes, work with human beings is complex, and education occurs within a web of social, organizational, and political contexts. Many of the factors that influence our students' circumstances lie outside our sphere of influence, and it is tempting to throw up our hands in defeat. There is no question that poverty, adverse childhood experiences, and chronic health problems negatively affect learning. Having said that, as teachers and administrators, there is much that we can positively influence:

- We can form positive suppositions about the future success of our students.

- We can provide high-quality instruction for them each and every day.
- We can support students' learning with linguistic and academic scaffolds to ensure full participation.
- We can actively work on establishing, maintaining, and repairing relationships with struggling students to create a safe and healthy learning space.
- We can devote our resources—time, attention, caring, and services—*unequally,* if that is what it takes, to meet the unequal needs of the students we teach.
- We can challenge ourselves to continually question whether current curricular, instructional, and organizational practices are sufficient to reach our students and support their success.

If you share these beliefs, then you're ready for this book. Providing students with access to the core curriculum; creating rich, culturally considerate learning experiences; setting high expectations; arranging for language development; and monitoring and guiding progress through formative assessment can change lives. We see the truth of this every day in the classrooms of caring educators who have made the commitment to reach students who are traditionally thought of as hard to teach. This book is filled with real-life stories of these excellent teachers and what they are doing to create learning opportunities for linguistically and culturally diverse students and others who struggle in school.

Excellent Instruction in Action

Let's drop in on a teacher who has embraced the five principles of effective instruction—middle school math teacher Alicia Gomez.

Mrs. Gomez previously taught at a school marked by apathy and low expectations; it was routine for the school to offer remedial classes for the high numbers of students not making academic progress. At her current school, which is located in a less affluent area of the city and enrolls a higher number of English learners and students with disabilities, things are different . . . and better. It's a vibrant, exciting place to work. Thanks to a deliberate effort to reach "hard-to-teach" culturally and linguistically diverse students with a history of academic struggle, there's been a positive effect on their performance and participation in school.

In her math classroom, Mrs. Gomez maintains a laserlike focus on high expectations and achievement. Her walls display pictures of successful individuals, both men and women, of various ethnicities and races. Her teaching style is oriented toward preventing learning gaps, and she does this by offering the kinds of academic and linguistic supports that we will discuss throughout this book. She believes that all her students can learn, because all her students *do* learn. But this doesn't "just happen"; it's a result of deliberate action she takes every day.

When Mrs. Gomez teaches a lesson on measuring angles with a protractor, her plans include the language supports that her English learners and struggling learners will need—such as a visual reference to words that will be part of her instruction. Today, she's written these words on a board at the front of the classroom: *angle, ray, acute, vertex, obtuse, right angle,* and $90°$. She asks her English learners how they say *angle* in their home languages and gets back many answers. She shows a right angle on the projector and writes $90°$ next to it as a review. "What do we call an angle that is less than 90 degrees?" she asks. "Please show me your answers on your whiteboards." All but three students write *acute*, and Mrs. Gomez points to the word *acute* on the classroom board to help the students who need it. When she asks what an angle greater than 90 degrees is called, she gestures to the word list again. It's a way to hint that the spelling of the word is there, but she doesn't give away the word. All students produce the correct answer, *obtuse*.

Once Mrs. Gomez finishes the terminology review, she puts a protractor on the projector and models how to line it up on the vertex of the right angle. She repeats the terms several times and prompts the class, "The first step is to place the protractor on the—" "Vertex!" the class responds.

Mrs. Gomez sets up her class in teams, and each team member is typically assigned a job during collaborative learning activities. Today's task is to measure a series of angles. One student lines up the protractor with each angle, another student measures the angle, and a third team member writes the answer on the worksheet. After each problem is completed, team members rotate responsibilities so that all are equally involved in the procedure. As they work, Mrs. Gomez circulates among the groups to check for understanding and accuracy, keeping an especially sharp eye on those compliant students who may not understand but pretend to in order to please the teacher. This type of close observation of student work allows her to assist those who might otherwise slip through the cracks.

Any time she judges that more guided instruction is needed to ensure understanding, she calls for the whole class's attention and models another problem on the projector. When all the teams have completed their collaborative worksheet, Mrs. Gomez distributes a second problem set for everyone to solve as an individual assessment of understanding. Again, she circulates through the room, looking over shoulders and checking in on the work. Although all the students demonstrate a general understanding of angle measurements, she notes that some will need more practice using the protractor and deciphering the measurements.

As a culminating activity, Mrs. Gomez asks students to briefly discuss why measuring angles is important. She encourages students to use their own experiences as a basis for their contributions to the discussion so that they realize the relationship between their life experiences and schooling.

Do you recognize aspects of Mrs. Gomez's approach in your own practices—or in those of other teachers in your school? She and her colleagues give every child an opportunity to learn. They have used the five principles of excellent instruction to figure out what works with hard-to-teach students and, in doing so, they've become the kind of teacher struggling students need. Over the next five chapters, we will explore the five principles and share more stories of great teachers putting these principles into action. And that's the key to this book—action.

Reading about good ideas is insufficient. Strengthening one's instructional effectiveness isn't a spectator sport. To that end, we have set up this book as a collection of actions that will help you transfer these principles from the page to your practice. The actions steps we recommend are short in terms of words, but they require thoughtful application and a willingness to interrogate your beliefs and practices.

We have ordered the chapters to align with a logical and practical progression of ideas—the best way, we think, to begin putting the principles to work for your students. Therefore we begin, like Mrs. Gomez, with a focus on expectations, then move to access, assessment, language instruction, and climate.

The Expectation of Success

Walk into Mario Cuéllar's 2nd grade classroom and you'll see the expectations he holds for his 28 students. His university pennant and degrees are posted, and so are captioned photographs of him as a youngster, each one describing a formative experience that shaped him as a learner. "Mr. Cuéllar's Learning Journey" is a favorite bulletin board with his students, who like seeing what their teacher looked like as a child. This isn't the only parallel he draws between himself and his students. For example, during morning calendar, he notes the days that he'll be attending class for the university master's program he is enrolled in. "I want the kids to see that I'm a learner like them, and that I face struggles that are similar to their own," he said.

Over the course of the school year, each child in Mr. Cuéllar's class develops a digital portfolio to document his or her own "learning journey." The teacher kicks off the project during the first week of school, conducting individual video interviews. Off camera, he asks questions to prompt discussion of identify and aspirations: "Who are you now, and who do you want to be?" Over the next nine months, the students take photographs and videos of themselves and selected classroom artifacts, and add audio to describe the significance of each item. For example, Nellie added a photograph of a math test she took and said, "I'm proud of this because it shows that I can solve problems. I used my math thinking to figure out how to measure shapes and find the area."

These digital portfolios are also a way for Mr. Cuéllar to maintain communication with the children's families. Parents receive an automated notification each time their child adds an item. "The parents really like this, and I do, too," Mr. Cuéllar said. "It gives them something positive to talk about at home. Families foster their child's aspirations, and this is a tool to help them do so. I encourage parents to add items as well, like photographs of their family reunion or the trip they took over the break to visit relatives. That helps me know more about their child."

In May, Mr. Cuéllar video-records the children as they watch the video of themselves from the first week of school, and he asks them to comment on the changes they see. Roberto said, "I'm taller and stronger! But I can see how much better of a reader I am. It was hard for me to read the intro statement card you gave me, but now it's super easy." Mr. Cuéllar asked, "How did that happen?" Roberto replied, "You helped me work hard at reading even though it's not my favorite subject. I like science best. You gave me lots of science things to read and then . . . I don't know . . . then I was a reader!"

The learning journey this 2nd grade teacher weaves through the year communicates his high expectations for his students as learners. He holds them to a standard and presumes all will succeed—even, and maybe especially, students like Roberto, whose reading progress was lagging behind after kindergarten and 1st grade. Mr. Cuéllar teaches at a school where each student's progress is shared in advance of the new school year. He was aware of Roberto's struggles before the first day of school. He also knew some things about Roberto's interests (science) and motivation (earning the respect of his peers), thanks to the assessments Roberto's 1st grade teacher had administered the previous spring. From the start, Mr. Cuéllar made sure to give Roberto plenty of science-oriented reading materials containing information his peers wouldn't know about. "Roberto became the authority in the classroom when it came to reptiles, space travel, and desert life," said the teacher.

Mr. Cuéllar also set high expectations for Nellie, a student with an identified math disability. He met frequently with her throughout the year for individual, needs-based instruction. "Nellie uses math manipulatives to boost her spatial awareness, because this is an area of difficulty for her," he explained. "It's a simple accommodation that allows her to keep pace with the math content standards for 2nd grade." To him, Nellie's math disability means "I just have to find the work-arounds."

What stands out to us in Mr. Cuéllar's approach is how active it is. Having high expectations does not mean telling students they're going to learn and then hoping for the best. Doug once had a neuroanatomy professor tell the class, "I don't know *how* you're going to learn this, but it's on the test." Doug thought to himself, "If my professor doesn't know how I'm going to learn it, what chance do I have?"

Too often, teachers make dangerous assumptions about what students can and cannot do. Putting too much stake in the power of positive thinking is one example, as when we tell students that they can do anything if they try hard enough. Unless we also provide these students with a clear path toward success, we're essentially asking them to rely on magical thinking, which has a very spotty track record. We're also shifting the burden to them; if their struggles persist, we can say to ourselves, "They must not have wanted it badly enough." It's dangerous to abdicate responsibility in this way, and it's dangerous to assume students who don't succeed are simply not putting enough effort in. But the even more dangerous assumption is that some children just aren't capable of doing the kind of work that their peers do. The language barrier is too high. Their past trauma is too severe.

The gaps in foundational skills are too great. They don't have the capacity for concentration they need to do the work.

Lowered expectations are seldom malicious. In fact, they often emerge from a place of compassion. We face a frustrated or bewildered child, and in a misguided attempt to rescue her, we tell her she doesn't have to do a critical part of the task. When we walk away, the child may initially be relieved and grateful. Over time, though, a destructive impression starts to form: "Other kids can do this, but not me. My teacher doesn't think I can do this, either. Why should I try, if I'm only going to fail?" Teaching with lowered expectations is teaching learned helplessness.

As teachers like Mr. Cuéllar know, setting expectations that will actually transform the classroom experiences of students who are used to struggling in school is a complex matter. It requires us to set out a clear pathway for success, disrupt patterns of behavior and mindset, and demonstrate to students that they *are* learners and their investment in learning is worthwhile. Here are the actions we recommend:

- Presume success.
- Teach with urgency.
- Communicate learning intentions, success criteria, and goals.
- Establish learning intentions that include both content and language.
- Foster student aspirations.

Presume Success

Working with students who are "harder to teach" begins and ends with our expectations. In later chapters we will examine instruction, assessment, and the learning climate, but these topics are meaningless unless we communicate that we expect students to achieve to a high standard. This is more difficult than it sounds.

All children can learn. We've all heard and read that statement so many times that it is little more than noise at this point.

What's more, in practice, all of us have seen behaviors of educators that betray this tenet. We've seen it in an administrator who refuses to support inclusive educational practices for students with disabilities. We've seen it in the guidance counselor who discourages a student from pursuing a rigorous course of study because "otherwise these kids don't graduate." We've seen it in the teacher who keeps the struggling readers in leveled texts that are well below grade level, thus failing to expose them to developmentally appropriate concepts. These practices, writ large and small, communicate unintended messages to the community about what we *really* believe about its children.

Failure is not an option. And yet, it is. According to the National Center for Educational Statistics, more than one million U.S. students drop out of high school each year (Kena et al., 2014). The evidence on dropout rates is that they disproportionately affect certain groups, especially black males, Hispanic males and females, and students with mild disabilities.

The road to dropping out of high school begins much earlier than high school. The likelihood that a child will leave high school without a diploma rises when he or she is retained, whether the retention decision is teacher-based or test-based (Huddleston, 2014). The path to failure is made clearer when a child who is already reading below grade level is kept in less challenging texts that further limit her learning of grade-level concepts, thereby leading to lower final grades. In fact, a study of 10 years of failure rates on the California High School Exit Exam, a high-stakes test of English language arts and mathematics knowledge required for graduation, found that grade point average was a strong predictor of failure (Zau & Betts, 2008). Did we mention that it was a child's grades in *4th grade* that correlated to her performance on a test six years later?

Teacher expectations of student success have a profound impact on a student's learning (Hattie, 2009). Our presumptions about their success should be assumptions about our own. In other words, what we believe about our students' potential is directly linked to what we believe about our own efficacy. The learning of students who come to school with all the prerequisites in place should not be the yardstick we use to measure our own teaching prowess. Those students are important and need our attention, of course, but quite frankly, a less skilled teacher will probably obtain similar results. But our collective ability to reach those hardest-to-teach students should be the evidence we point to with pride: *I taught him when others had given up on him.* The impact on a student's learning, both short-term and long-term, should be an important factor in assessing our own teaching.

Teachers communicate our presumptions about students' success when we set goals with them and encourage them to self-assess. We build a growth mindset with children when we use language that strengthens their understanding about the link between effort and results (Dweck, 2006). And we support success when we build a failure-friendly classroom that fosters academic risk taking (Miller, 2015). Children and adolescents deserve to interact with adults at school who believe in their capacity to learn, even when they themselves have doubts. Presuming success provides a starting point and ending point for our work, and it guides every point in between.

Teach with Urgency

Over time, the malaise fostered by learned helplessness begins to permeate the larger learning environment, spreading like a virus to other students. Older students, now tracked into remedial middle and high school courses, have perfected task avoidance, and their teachers respond in kind, slowing down their instruction. They don't teach with urgency, because what's the point of pressing? Everyone will just do what they can comfortably do, and that's perfectly OK.

Early in a partnership with a large high school with a track record of low student achievement and a significant dropout rate,

Doug conducted a time sample study of use of instructional minutes (Fisher, 2009). He discovered that in remedial classrooms, an average of 13 percent of the instructional minutes were lost to taking attendance, housekeeping, and unstructured time at the beginning and end of the class period. Now let's do the math: The state department of education requires 54,000 instructional minutes. A loss of 13 percent translates into is 7,020 minutes— 117 fewer hours of instruction in a single year. At a time when many are advocating for longer instructional days and school years, it seems prudent to first consider whether the minutes currently allocated are being used wisely. On a happy note, the principal of this high school used the results of Doug's time study to introduce an initiative he called "the Opportunity to Learn standard," which helped the school vastly reduce noninstructional time and increase student engagement in academic tasks.

The name of this school's initiative reminds us that opportunity to learn (OTL) is about students' exposure to rigorous and challenging content. There is a tremendous, well-documented OTL deficit gap within U.S. classrooms among English learners, students with disabilities, and those working below grade level (Abedi, Leon, & Kao, 2008). This is especially troubling given the relationship between OTL and student achievement. One study of this relationship noted that lower rates of OTL in class accounted for 32 percent of the variance in student achievement growth scores for students with disabilities in general education classrooms (Elliott, 2015). In other words, a student's presence in a busy classroom is not a sufficient measure of their engagement with learning tasks. Those hardest-to-teach students need to be carefully monitored and refocused when needed to ensure that they are receiving maximal opportunities to learn.

Mr. Cuéllar, the 2nd grade teacher whose story opened this chapter, keeps a small, framed plaque on his desk that reads, *As fast as we can; as slow as we must.* It's his reminder to himself that he needs to teach his students with urgency. "There's not a minute to waste in this classroom," he tells them. "Your journey begins with all of us believing that our time together is sacred time." He checks in more frequently with students like Nellie and Roberto, who can drift away from learning tasks, whether it's by taking a more passive role in group work or hesitating to start independent work. He also dedicates an unequal amount of his time to teacher-directed instruction with these and other students who need higher levels of support. "These children are already behind," he said. "I'm the catalyst that can accelerate their learning. My expectations need to be even higher for them to get them moving toward success."

What does a teaching with urgency look like? According to Principal Brian Henderson, "You know it when you see it. Some classrooms have a buzz about them that communicates a sense of urgency. It's not like there is desperation or undue stress. Teachers can make learning urgent without making the class-room a pressure cooker."

Urgency is necessary, but frenzy is harmful. Negative emotions such as anxiety, fear, and embarrassment form an affective filter than can constrain language development and undermine learning. At the same time, the classroom needs to convey to students that there is important work to do. Achieving this bal-ance of "welcoming" and "serious" supports the success of all students but is especially critical for students who are hard to teach. Although they need a safe learning environment where it's OK to take risks, they also need to feel *inclined* to take those risks—drawn to do so because they see learning as a compel-ling and worthwhile goal. When it comes to communicating the urgency for learning, there are three important actions to take. We'll explore them now.

Manage lesson pace

When lessons are too slow, it signals to students that what they're doing isn't very important. A lesson that's too rushed sends a similar message. Managing the pace of a lesson is a matter of looking for evidence that the pace you've set is appropriate. If students are interested in the lesson and you see that they understand and are not off task, then the pace is probably about right. If the pace is too slow, you will see students stare at you or off into space, and the air in the room will start to feel heavier and heavier. Here are some pace-management strategies to employ during planning and during lessons.

Find an aspect of the content that interests you. If the content is boring to you, it's going to be boring to students. If you are enthusiastic, then your students will likely be interested, especially if you can connect it to their lives. Make sure that you have found your own way to connect with the content; then consider the various ways you can make the content relevant for students and their own experiences.

Use a timer. Telling students they have 5 minutes to complete a task and then letting the task time go for 8 or 10 minutes sends the message that time isn't very important and that students should feel free to work at their own pace. When students are "on the clock," they are more likely to focus on the task at hand. A prominently displayed timer helps students monitor their pace and take more responsibility for timely task completion. There are a number of timers available for free download.

Manage materials. Having materials at hand allows for efficient use of time and sends the message to students that the work they'll be doing is important. You've planned this learning experience; it's not just something you've thrown together.

Smooth transitions. Allowing lots of time between various aspects of the lesson can also be a source of diminished urgency. Smooth transitions allow students to stay focused and make connections between different tasks in the learning sequence. Try restating the learning intention during transitions and set up predictable routines.

Provide visual and verbal instructions. To keep more students focused on their learning, present task instructions in both visual and verbal formats. If students have to rely on only one or the other, some students will be lost and will need information repeated, slowing down the lesson.

Check for understanding. Throughout each lesson, regularly pause to see if and how well students understand the content. This can be as simple as asking everyone to show a thumbs-up if they are with you and a thumbs-down if they are not. As we will discuss in greater detail in the chapter on assessment, there are a number of ways to check in with students. Doing so can signal an effectively paced lesson.

Maximize lesson time

Teaching with urgency means using every minute of the class time available. Delaying the start of class for administrative details signals to students that learning can wait—and there's no real need to be there on time. Ending class early and providing "free time" before the bell communicates that there is time to waste and that learning isn't important enough to require the entire period.

With a little planning time and some procedural habit building, you can keep students engaged in meaningful tasks from the outset of the allotted time all the way to the next bell. We find that getting off to an immediate, learning-focused start is critical. In some classes, this is a quick-write prompt; in other classes, it is a challenge. In still other classes, there is a reading to be completed or a math problem to solve.

Middle school math teacher Haley Spencer starts every day with "minute math," with students racing against themselves and their teacher to see who can solve the most review problems in 60 seconds. Her students race to her class to play the game. Elementary school teacher Crystal Brooks starts her class journal writing each day using timed writing prompts that students use later in the day for editing. In both cases, these teachers have ways to ensure that students are focused on learning from the very moment they enter the classroom.

Use wait time

It may seem strange to include a conversation about wait time in a section on urgency. After all, waiting could communicate to students that the lesson isn't very important. In fact, the opposite is true. When teachers provide appropriate wait time for students, it signals that their thinking is valuable and that waiting for them to share is worthwhile.

The concept of "wait time" was invented by Mary Budd Rowe in the early 1970s and refined over the next 15 years. Rowe (1987) found that giving students three or more seconds of undisturbed wait time led to a number of positive outcomes:

- The length and correctness of their responses increased.
- The number of "I don't know" and no-answer responses decreased.
- The number of volunteered responses from other students increased.
- Scores on achievement tests increased.

Rowe found that the implementation of wait time changed teacher behavior as well. Most significantly, when they asked fewer questions, those questions were of higher quality. Teachers who provide adequate wait time for students tend to ask more complex questions, including questions that require synthesis and evaluation.

Rowe noted several different types of wait time, two of which have become common practice and are critical for students who struggle with school (Atwood & Wilen, 1991). The first, often called *wait time 1*, occurs after the teacher has asked a question or posed a problem. If a student is ready to respond, she should be encouraged to do so. But if a student doesn't answer, the teacher should wait at least three seconds (some people argue that five seconds is better) before turning to another student or providing additional prompts and cues. The second, often called *wait time 2*, occurs after a student has responded. When teachers wait just two seconds after a student stops speaking, students are much more likely to extend their responses, self-correct if needed, and ask follow-up questions. Waiting for students to respond and providing appropriate scaffolds when they do communicates that their responses are important.

Wait time is particularly relevant for English learners who require additional time to process language in English—their non-native tongue. Some may need to translate the question mentally and formulate an answer before responding. In reality, they have double the work and benefit from additional time.

Communicate Learning Intentions, Success Criteria, and Goals

Findings in cognitive-behavioral sciences tell us that students' understanding of the learning destination, coupled with goals to reach an end point, is a "major condition of learning" and "it helps considerably if students share a commitment and sense of engagement to these goals" (Hattie, 2009, p. 32). In other words, the importance of giving students an explicit picture of the outcomes they are working toward cannot be overstated. All students, but especially those who struggle with the content and academic language of the discipline, benefit from clear learning intentions and success criteria that provide a map for meeting expectations and help them set and pursue goals.

First, let's quickly review the terms. A *learning intention* or *objective* lets students know what they will be learning today. *Success criteria* capture the observable and measureable outcomes of the learning—what the teacher will be looking for in their work and, critically, what they should look for in their own work. For example, the learning intention in 8th grade social studies class might be "to describe the three branches of government and their major functions," while the success criteria communicated to students would be "You'll know you've accomplished this when you write three paragraphs naming each branch and describing at least two functions of each." With this information clear to them, students can set goals for themselves or with assistance. A short-term goal for this task might be to complete a bulleted list of the branches and their functions and have it checked by a peer by the end of the class period.

Identifying the observable and measurable criteria that will be used to make judgments about learning is a necessary part of communicating high expectations. Moreover, it provides students with the ability to judge their own work.

We believe that establishing a daily purpose through clear learning intentions and relevance (not just long-term unit intentions) assists students in understanding how what they are doing in class each day incrementally advances their learning. Too often we find students who have no idea how the content from Tuesday's lesson relates to Thursday's. Daily content and language learning intentions prevent these students from experiencing learning as a series of disjointed activities.

Further, a clear learning intention and success criteria allow for an examination of the grade-level expectations for students. When teachers design lesson after lesson that are below grade level, students have little chance to accelerate their progress. When Jana was a special education teacher at a large inner-city high school—in the days before standards—the reading materials were skills-based, fill-in-the-blanks books. Although these were generally aligned the students' reading levels—most of her students were reading at the 2nd, 3rd, and 4th grade levels—they also seemed to be written for 2nd, 3rd, and 4th graders rather than for adolescents. The lowest-level book even had "My name is _____" printed at the top of every page.

Understanding how demoralizing these materials were for the teenagers she was teaching, Jana purchased a book of abridged classic tales (e.g., *The Tell-Tale Heart*, *A Tale of Two Cities*) that included vocabulary and comprehension exercises for each story. Her students accessed the text through read-aloud and choral reading, and Jana provided differentiation during the follow-up activities. With rapt attention, these students engaged in the work, and the discussions they had were rich and age-appropriate. They were able to complete assignments previously assumed to be beyond their level. One day, a beaming student announced to his classmates that the story they were reading was also being read in Honors English.

The lesson here is that keeping underperforming students at their current level, especially when it is far below grade level, doesn't serve them well. Of course some small-group or individualized instruction should focus on closing the gaps between their current performance and the expectation for their same peers, but if that's the only instruction they receive, they will continue to perform below grade level. All students deserve instruction that is aligned with grade-level standards, and a quick review of a week's worth of learning targets will reveal patterns that may signal a need to ramp up expectations.

Establish Learning Intentions That Include Both Content and Language

Darnell Browning, a middle school science teacher, draws first and foremost on his state's content frameworks to guide his instruction and craft his learning intentions for students. He uses essential questions to frame these learning intentions and increase cognitive coherence. His current essential question from the framework is, "How do organisms change over time in response to changes in the environment?" As part of this unit, his students will conduct a short investigation to locate information about an endangered or threatened species in their state. Here are the content learning intentions for the first day's lesson, phrased to position students as active participants in the learning:

Today I will (1) investigate a topic using multiple resources, (2) analyze and interpret data, and (3) provide evidence for conclusions.

Mr. Browning also furnishes success criteria for the lesson:

By the end of the period, I will have completed an information organizer about my selected species.

Because some of the students in his classes are English learners, Mr. Browning also consults his state's English language development standards, which systematically address various aspects of academic language learning in his discipline. Mr. Browning has analyzed the language demands of the tasks that students need to complete during the lesson, such as using descriptive language, making comparisons, and using if/then sentences. These language learning intentions fall into several categories (Echevarría et al., 2017; Fisher & Frey, 2011; Short & Echevarría, 2016). They are essential for English learners but also very useful for native English speakers who struggle:

- *Academic vocabulary use* of specialized and technical terms
- *Language function* (e.g., describe, explain, inquire, express opinions, pose and respond to questions)
- *Language structure* (e.g., sequencing events, using superlative adjectives and conditional verbs, using correct noun-verb agreements)
- *Language learning strategies* (e.g., student self-correction, self-monitoring and prereading)

Discipline-specific vocabulary use is often the focus of Mr. Browning's language learning intentions, but other language functions are typically practiced in each lesson. Here are the language learning intentions for the lesson:

I will (1) engage in collaborative discussions using the key vocabulary: *endangered, ecosystem, interpret;* (2) report findings citing evidence for conclusions; and (3) use superlative adjectives in the written report.

To establish a purpose for learning in his students' minds, Mr. Browning begins each lesson by posting and discussing his content and language learning intentions and the success criteria for the lesson. He posts all of these on the whiteboard and on his learning management system (LMS) workspace where students will conduct this investigation. He also reviews them intermittently with individual students throughout the period. "I've learned they're more successful when they know what the learning intentions are," he said. "When I'm clear about what they're learning and how they're going to use the knowledge, I'm better at assessing, too." Posting and reviewing the learning intentions and success criteria helps Mr. Browning focus his instruction and assessment, and perhaps more importantly, it allows students to see the purpose of the lesson, the language they are learning, and what they are expected to accomplish. Mr. Browning has seen that when he makes learning transparent for students, they are more engaged in the lessons. In this lesson, students focus on the topic through investigation of information but also have multiple language-practice opportunities. Identifying the language learning intentions ensures that students will use academic terms and also appropriate language forms. In addition, Mr. Browning posts language frames with superlative terms as a resource for students who need it (e.g., great/greater/greatest; little/less/least).

His daily learning intentions have a cumulative effect in creating a sense of urgency in his students. "I'm very task-oriented," he said. "I want my students to see that scientific thinking is about engaging in the work and investigation that marks the field. Everyone likes to say, 'We're learning to think like scientists,' but that doesn't truly happen until you begin to formulate questions, investigate phenomena, and test hypotheses throughout the day, not just when you're here with me." To clarify the long view, Mr. Browning posts all his daily content, language learning, intentions, and related success criteria on a digital calendar at the start of every unit. "It helps them to see the logical progression of concepts and the tasks related to them," he said. "Each day I revisit the calendar and have them check off tasks they're completing in the unit." In doing so, he builds a task-oriented mindset for his students about their own learning.

Foster Student Aspirations

To our thinking, school is not about test scores or even becoming college and career ready; it's about giving young people an opportunity to clarify and realize their aspirations. The expectations we hold for our students are ultimately just an intermediate step to them holding expectations for themselves. Hattie (2009) reports that students' expectations of themselves, and their self-assessments of their progress, have a significant impact on their learning. But how do we build a student's personal expectations? It's a matter of focusing them, throughout their educational careers, on two major, essential questions: "Who do you want to be?" and "What do you want to be?"

For students who struggle with school, asking these two questions can make all the difference in the world. Let's take the questions apart to see how they can guide the interactions students have with educational experiences.

Answering "Who do you want to be?" requires that students evaluate their social and behavioral selves and consider changes necessary to become the best version of themselves that they can be. Getting them to engage with the question might start with conversations about pride, kicked off with questions like, "When do you feel proud of yourself, inside or outside school?" When Ricky was in 5th grade, he told us that he was proud when he played soccer. When we asked him why, he never said anything about winning or being a professional player; he talked about being the captain of the team. Ricky wanted to be a leader. On days when Ricky was acting as his best self, his teacher talked with him about leadership and what leadership might look like in the classroom. He helped Ricky draw these connections and start to manage his behavior so that it was consistent with the person he wanted to be.

Older students also have to figure out who they want to be. Lizbeth was a bully to younger students, but she prided herself in being a "nice girl" who had a lot of friends. After several conversations, Nancy asked her, "What obstacle is holding you back right now? How can you be the person you're supposed to be?" Lizbeth said that she felt that other people were getting more attention and that she was jealous. What was a fairly problematic situation was resolved when Lizbeth took responsibility for her actions and cut out those that were not consistent with who she wanted to be.

The second important question—"What do you want to be?"—prompts students to consider their professional futures. Too many students are unaware of all they might do, simply because their schools (and families) have not exposed them to the wide range of jobs and careers that exist in the world. Further, some have career goals that are a significant stretch and haven't thought seriously about what obtaining these dreams jobs would require. We have lost count of the number of students who first tell us that they want to be rappers and professional athletes. Jason, an English learner struggling in 11th grade, told us he wanted to be a doctor for a few years and then, when he saved up some money, he would become a soccer player. When asked how long he thought it took to become a doctor, Jason said, "A couple of years." When asked about the grade point average and SAT requirements for college admission, Jason had no idea. When we don't focus students on aspirations and appropriate expectations, the results can be false hope, crushed dreams, and chronic disengagement.

Conversation with students is a great way to provide this guidance. Here are some key questions and prompts you might want to include (Smith, Fisher, & Frey, 2015):

1. What do you like to do, and can that be a career?

2. How do people who do that for a living prepare for this career?
3. Let's find out what you need to do in middle school/high school to put you on that path.
4. Are you on track to reach this goal?
5. Let's make a plan to reach your goals.

We are reminded of Arturo, a 9th grade student recently exited from special education services who was failing math and barely passing his other classes. When asked the question "What do you want to be?" he answered, "An architect." When asked, "On a scale of 1 to 10, with 10 being absolutely sure and there is nothing else you want to be, how sure are you that you want to be an architect?" Arturo responded, "Ten!" The discussions that ensued focused on the role of mathematics in architecture as well how understanding history, being skilled in science, and being a proficient writer are necessary to be successful in the field. Arturo had never considered that his current classes were preparing him for this vocation. These short conversations did not suddenly result in Arturo earning perfect grades, but they did fire up his internal motivation. He started to attend an after-school program to make up his assignments, and he ended up passing every class that year. Any time Arturo was faced with a daunting or difficult task, he'd repeat the mantra, "I have to do it, because I'm going to be an architect." But not all students know what they want to be, much less who they want to be or how to get there. In those cases, educators have to ensure that students are exposed to a wide range of experiences that broaden horizons and expand the range of possibilities. There are a number of ways to do this:

- Assign texts about people who have made a difference and people with different roles in society.
- Use planned field trips to visit places that highlight more of the important jobs and careers they might want to explore.

- Create a college-going culture in which students know their grade point averages and the course of study required for college admission.
- Match students with mentors who can help them investigate the requirements of careers that interest them.
- Provide internship opportunities for students to try out different jobs and roles.

Remember, too, that our students today will be entering a workforce that will consist of jobs we haven't even conceived of yet. Keep an eye out for information about new inventions and innovations, and share these learnings with students, who might just be sparked with an idea that will change the world.

• • •

Having high expectations for hard-to-teach students is a key component in turning them toward success. We are reminded of sociologist Jane Elliott's classic "Blue Eyes/Brown Eyes" exercise. In the original, controversial study, the researcher told a group of young blue-eyed and brown-eyed students that people with blue eyes are superior. These children went on to act as if they *were* superior, speaking up more in class, displaying more self-confidence, and actually scoring higher on tests. In stage 2, the researcher told the children that she had been wrong and that *brown-eyed people* were actually superior. She watched as the brown-eyed children in the class stepped up to become leaders and performed better on tests. It's a classic example of the power of expectations.

Access to the Core Curriculum

The 10th grade biology class had been tasked with designing a water filtration system to clean the polluted water their teacher had given them. Students worked in groups of four or five, consulting short technical documents about design principles. Each group worked with a kit of supplies that included coffee filters, sand, pebbles, tubing, and rubber bands. The groups also had data tables to record the results of their experiment and probeware to measure the temperature, turbidity, and pH of their filtered water. Lastly, they were furnished with water quality charts that took all of these factors into account.

Several students in the class required a differentiated experience in order to fully access the task. An English learner, Jovelyn, was placed in a group with a fluent native language speaker to serve as a language broker. From time to time, Jovelyn and Marisol could be overheard conversing in their shared Tagalog language. At another table, Kiera, a student with an intellectual disability, was in a group that used a smartpen to record the conversations that took place as they built the filtration system and collected data. These recordings and notes would later be uploaded to the class learning management system (LMS) so

Kiera could refer back to them. Finally, throughout the room were several students who performed well below grade level. The teacher, Alice Ononiwu, provided copies of parallel technical documents that she had altered to include shorter sentences and a glossary for the more challenging vocabulary. All of the aforementioned budding biologists benefited from the sentence starters for the lab report that their teacher had posted on the LMS, along with a content and grammar checklist for finalizing their work.

Importantly, Ms. Ononiwu had designed this lab experiment with her struggling students in mind. She selected the water filtration lesson after speaking with Jovelyn, who had described her own experiences when she had inconsistent access to potable water after a hurricane. Kiera's assistive technology plan had just recently been updated at her IEP meeting two weeks ago, and the teacher was seeking opportunities to use it so both she and Kiera could learn more about using a smartpen. At the beginning of the year, the enhanced technical documents, sentence starters, and checklists were initially offered only to specific students, but Ms. Ononiwu had abandoned that practice in the first quarter. "I saw that there were lots of kids who would choose to use, or not use, these items. It dawned on me that they were perfectly capable of differentiating some things for themselves," she explained.

What this biology teacher knows is what many of us have had to find out over time. Students who have not been academically successful in the past are not going to suddenly make progress just because we want them to. Yes, it is necessary to set and communicate high expectations for all students, but that doesn't mean we can turn a blind eye to individual student needs. We want students with a history of academic struggle to be on the learning highway with everyone else, and we have to build the ramps that will get them there. In other words, they need access to the core curriculum, and our role is to deliver the instruction and differentiation that makes access possible.

In this chapter, we will discuss actionable items that give hard-to-teach students the "all-access passes" they need to accelerate their pace of learning. As we've established, your English learners, students receiving special education services, students living in poverty or experiencing trauma, and students with a history of academic struggle don't need remedial classes. They need the same kind of rigorous coursework that others students thrive with. But they also need instructional and curricular scaffolds that apprentice them into the self-sustaining habits of learning that are essential for all. Here are the actions we recommend:

- Focus on providing high-quality instruction.
- Differentiate instruction.
- Use accommodations and modifications as needed.

Focus on Providing High-Quality Instruction

Every teacher sets out to provide high-quality instruction, but not all of us achieve it. As with any goal, defining the desired outcome can help chart a course forward. So what is *high-quality instruction*, anyway?

As we define it, high-quality instruction is aligned with the content standards and includes a number of nonnegotiable parts or aspects, especially focused instruction that includes learning intentions and teacher modeling, guided instruction that includes scaffolds, and collaborative learning that allows students to consolidate their understanding with peers (Fisher et al., 2016). A teacher does not employ these parts in any set order, nor can the process of using them be easily scripted. That's because high-quality instruction is always delivered in response to students' understandings, misunderstandings, and errors. In other words, it's a recursive process in which students are engaged in learning tasks that will usher them toward the next expected outcome.

The non-negotiable aspects of high-quality instruction are elucidated in the FIT Teaching approach developed by Doug and Nancy (see Fisher et al., 2016). As you will see, high-quality instruction for English learners in particular includes the components of SIOP, as described by Jana and her colleagues (e.g., Echevarría et al., 2017). The two approaches *fit* together nicely.

Communicate expectations and relevance

The first essential we want to talk about is clearly communicating learning intentions and success criteria to all students. Because we have discussed expectations in Chapter 1, we won't repeat ourselves here except to stress that providing students with a clear picture of what they are learning and why they are learning it is especially essential for those with a history of struggle in school. These students can be unsure of what to pay attention to or how to meet their teacher's expectations. Reiterating clear learning intentions throughout every lesson keeps them grounded and helps them grasp why the work they're doing matters. Note, too, that students need to *experience* this relevance. When creating lesson plans, this means designing tasks that immerse students in the information, strategies, ideas, and skills they need to fully engage with the content.

Provide cognitive and linguistic modeling

A second essential component of high-quality instruction is modeling—teachers metaphorically opening up our brains and sharing thinking with students about how we are engaging with content. It can and should be done at various points in a lesson. Cognitive and linguistic modeling provides students a glimpse into how someone else is thinking about a complex idea or a complex text. It's a way to apprentice students into more expert thinking and expose them to academic language use. Further, teachers should routinely use modeling to scaffold students' understanding, especially in response to errors that are uncovered. Rather than simply correct an incorrect response or explain the right answer, teachers providing high-quality instruction intentionally shift cognitive responsibility to students.

Incorporate collaborative learning

Another non-negotiable aspect of good instruction is collaborative learning. All students, and in particular those who struggle with learning and language, benefit from spending significant amounts of time engaged with peers in collaborative learning. In fact, we have argued that about 50 percent of the instructional minutes averaged across a week should involve student-to-student interactions (e.g., Frey, Fisher, & Nelson, 2013). This 50-percent target frees the teacher to provide additional systematic and intentional instruction to students who need it, including language instruction (see Chapter 4). Note that when classrooms are always quiet places focused narrowly on lecture and independent work, it's hard to integrate the academic language experiences that can be so beneficial for students who struggle. Simply put, nobody gets better at something that they don't do. To make progress, students learning English and students with a history of academic struggle need significant amounts of guided practice.

Differentiate Instruction

The students we teach bring a wealth of experiences, interests, and levels of readiness to the classroom. This variety makes our work engaging but also challenging. While all of us acknowledge the presence of a range of learners within our classrooms, and almost all of us are working in schools with evaluation systems that place a high value on responsive and adaptive teaching practices, many teachers still view student variance as "problematic, and view integrating these differences into lesson planning as a time-consuming task" (Smit & Humpert, 2012, p. 1153). It's a discouraging finding, as it suggests that far too many students are not getting the opportunity to learn they need and deserve.

If you hope to reach a wide range of students—struggling ones in particular—you must differentiate your instruction. The SIOP Model, for example, offers proven ways to help students access the curriculum and improve achievement (Echevarría et al., 2017; Short et al., 2011), including an approach to differentiating instruction for English learners and students who struggle academically.

The practice of differentiating instruction is predicated on anticipating the need for adaptive teaching and using formative assessment practices and feedback to accelerate student progress (Tomlinson, 2001). It is not, as is sometimes misinterpreted, something that you "do" after you have planned the unit of study. Differentiation begins with considering the range of student interests, readiness, and their overall learning profiles (such as background experiences, language, and culture), all of which influence the ways students learn. These student- and home-related factors have a profound influence on learning success and failure, and failing to plan with these in mind will limit students' achievement (Hattie, 2009). The teacher's aim, then, is to craft instruction that considers student interest, readiness, and learning profile as critical components.

As Tomlinson (2001) explains, differentiation can be applied to three curricular elements: content, process, and product.

- *Content* is what we teach—the information and ideas that students engage with as they work toward learning goals— and is derived primarily from grade-level standards. The learning progressions now found in standards documents can be instructive in this regard, as they outline expectations across grade bands rather than within a single grade.

- *Process* describes how students will learn the content, and it centers on the activities teachers use—reading assignments, hands-on exploration, collaborative research, discussion, and so on.
- *Product* is the means for students to demonstrate the learning progress they are making and, eventually, their content mastery. Think of "product" as the assignments we use both formatively and summatively to assess students and plan for future instruction.

Regardless of the curricular element being differentiated, communication and feedback from the teacher is a vital component of the differentiation process and is necessary to move students forward in their learning. This feedback should also enlist the learner as an active participant in his or her learning. Figure 3.1 illustrates practices commonly associated with differentiating content, process, and product. Let's take a closer look at how these practices support struggling students by improving their access to the curriculum.

FIGURE 3.1
Examples of Content, Process, and Product Differentiation

Content	Process	Product
Using adaptive learning software that adjusts based on student responses	Designing a range of tiered assignments that call for increasingly sophisticated skill application, progressing toward mastery	Assigning homework that requires more or less time to complete or requires different levels of skill application
Employing a flipped classroom approach that provides some students with additional background information in advance of face-to-face instruction	Providing oral and written feedback tailored to the student's level of understanding	Creating open tasks that can be carried out in multiple ways

FIGURE 3.1 *(continued)*

Examples of Content, Process, and Product Differentiation

Content	Process	Product
Using leveled texts in reading instruction	Using peer review processes for ongoing tasks, and allowing students to revise their work	Setting up choice boards that include required assignments and student choice items
Pre-testing to locate knowledge gaps	Allowing time for additional practice	Using Role-Audience-Format-Topic (RAFT) writing assignments
Incorporating student interests and experiences into assignment to increase relevance	Developing review and study guides to reinforce new learning	Employing graduated rubrics to guide and evaluate a range of learners
Creating learning stations designed to build student background knowledge and increase their practice time with content	Providing a graphic organizer as an intermediate device to assist the student in organizing concepts and connections	Developing goal-setting agreements and accompanying learning contracts with individual students
Assigning readings that are conceptually linked but tailored to a range of reading proficiencies	Modeling and thinking aloud as you teach	Providing a menu of assignment options students can use to demonstrate mastery
Using essential questions to build relevance and foster connections	Reading aloud texts as needed to increase listening comprehension	Providing Genius Hour opportunities for students to explore and act upon what inspires them

Differentiate content tasks

Effective task design—charting an instructional course that will lead all students to content mastery—is a critical part of teaching. The goal is to provide a range of ways that students can engage with the content, helping to ensure every student will be able to process, understand, and eventually independently apply new skills and understandings. As an instructional practice, differentiation aligns with principles of learning that identify moderate challenge as the key to progress. Tasks that are too difficult can halt learning and discourage the learner; tasks that are too easy fail to motivate or bring about positive change.

There are all kinds of complex tasks you might incorporate in your lessons. In order to help your students connect to content, it's important to examine what various tasks would ask them to do and then figure out how each might be differentiated to better accommodate student readiness, interest, and learning profiles. Some students, especially those who are the focus of this book, need additional scaffolding, support, or instruction in order to engage with and master the tasks you present. Let's take a look at some common task types and what differentiating them entails.

Decision tasks require students to apply criteria to make a selection from a range of possibilities. Differentiating such tasks requires the teacher to consider a wider range of activity options for students to choose from and teach students about the criteria they can use to make selections.

For example, Daniel Carlson's 6th grade social studies students were assigned a decision task in which they had to select examples and nonexamples of present-day laws with origins in the Code of Hammurabi. They read an informational text, conducted Internet research, and discussed their findings with team members. Several students in the class needed additional supports to engage in this task. Mr. Carlson met with them in a small group (he calls it a huddle) and reviewed the text with them while the rest of the class read independently. He reminded them to annotate the text as they read it. In addition, Mr. Carlson compiled a set of Internet resources and encouraged everyone to explore them via a student-friendly search engine, kidzsearch. com, which imports Simple English Wikipedia entries and edits them for a school audience.

Similarly, 9th grade English teacher Mick Quinn's students had finished Chapter 2 of Jack London's *The Call of the Wild*. He asked his students to return to the text and identify examples of the psychological and physical shock endured by the book's protagonist, farm dog Buck, in his new life as a sled dog in Alaska. Mr. Quinn ensured content access for two students with disabilities by providing a Universal Design for Learning (UDL) digital version of the book. These students used the digital version's hyperlinks to look up unfamiliar words, phrases, terms, and locations, and ultimately, the students were able to find the necessary text evidence and complete the task alongside their peers.

Judgment tasks require students to consider what they have read or learned thus far in order to predict what will occur next. Differentiating judgment tasks requires the teacher to consider both the pacing of the lesson, so that predictions are appropriate, and the instruction students need to be able make inferences about texts and tasks.

For example, the 11th grade environmental science students in Kenya Montrose's class read an excerpt from Rachel Carson's *Silent Spring*, a work often credited with launching the environmental movement. They made predictions about what they would find in two reviews written at the time of publication, one critical and the other full of praise for the book. Several students predicted that reviews would stress the book's potential to educate people about the environment. Others thought this aspect would be ignored because, as Nichole put it, "Nobody was taking care of the environment back then; just look at what happened." Ms. Montrose used these predictions as the basis for comparing the two reviews. For the five students in her class who would benefit from additional supports, she had made copies of the articles with additional prompts inserted to remind them "stop and think" or to make a note of a position stated by the reviewer.

Problem tasks require students to resolve conflicting information in order to determine a decision path that will lead them to a single outcome. They are a mainstay of the mathematics classroom and are used by teachers who want students to read across multiple texts. Extended word problems often feature information that is not relevant, and at times may even suggest an incorrect line of reasoning. However, the end product is well defined, as there is usually a single correct answer. Differentiating problem tasks requires the teacher to find and present resources that are not only comprehensible to students but also include conflicting information as well as ambiguity.

Fifth grade teacher Joseph Cisse challenged his students to solve complex mathematics problems by presenting teams of students with several pieces of text they could use to create a scenario: a monthly household electricity statement, a list of the family's major appliances and their energy ratings, and the electric company's new time-of-day pricing plan that discounts usage during off-peak hours. Each team worked together to propose a plan for the family that would result in the greatest overall savings. Importantly, this problem task required students to read closely and for detail, and to go back to consult the texts repeatedly.

Mr. Cisse made sure that his hardest-to-teach students were members of different groups so that peer supports could be used more equitably. In addition, Mr. Cisse had met with these same students earlier in the day to frontload information about how the billing statements were deciphered. He also reviewed the three previously taught methods for calculating the costs, then asked each student to determine which method they would use. By the time the extended activity began, these students were prepared to engage in the task.

Fuzzy tasks are vaguely defined in terms of their initial purpose, and they possess all of the features of the tasks mentioned previously: the need to make multiple decisions, choose from multiple paths, and arrive at multiple outcomes. The biology lab experiment profiled at the beginning of the chapter is a fuzzy task. Problem-based learning is built on resolving fuzzy tasks. As such, they are better suited for end-of-unit or culminating projects, after a strong knowledge base has been built. Differentiating fuzzy tasks requires the teacher to consider students' metacognitive skills as well as the materials that they will need to engage in these types of tasks.

For example, Ms. Montrose, the environmental sciences teacher, gave each team of students an imaginary $5,000 budget to create a plan for raising awareness about sustainable resources in their community. The students had studied xeriscaping, soft path water conservation, solar and wind energy generation, and green technologies, and they were equipped to engage in this task. One team wrote a plan for producing a public service announcement (PSA) on the importance of replacing invasive exotic species with native plants and made a prototype film. Another team developed an audio message on driving habits that increase gas mileage that would automatically play at fuel pumps while customers filled up.

Ms. Montrose met with Bernard, whose group was making the PSA. She gave him a script outline with prompts to determine the scenario, goal, reasons, and facts and to provide more information (see http://www.readwritethink.org/files/resources/script_outline.pdf). This additional information allowed Bernard to lead the planning discussion within his group and move their project forward. "Bernard doesn't have as much experience leading conversations like this, so the additional content gave him the confidence to do so," his teacher explained. Ms. Montrose also checked in with some students each day to monitor their progress and make a plan for the following day. These daily plans included a task goal (e.g., "By the end of class today, I'll have gas-savings calculations ready for my group to include in our audio message") and a status check-in near the end of the period. "At this point in the year, most of the students can operate successfully as individuals and teams. But a few of them need more frequent check-ins to keep them moving forward," she said. This is an example of a process support, which we will discuss in more detail in the next section.

Differentiate learning processes

To ensure all students can access the curriculum, we also need to interrogate the processes we're asking them to engage in. Long gone are the days when people assumed "teaching" meant "dispensing information"; simply telling students everything they need to know is patently ineffective and a waste of time. Learning happens through doing, and effective teaching means creating experiences for students that give them reliable interaction with the curriculum. For students who are struggling, the means of engagement can be the difference between success and failure.

Differentiating process is about ensuring your instruction provides multiple ways for students to acquire and consolidate knowledge. For instance, a teacher might use a reading assignment to introduce students to a new concept and differentiate that process for variations in language and reading readiness by incorporating opportunities for students to collaborate with one another and discuss concepts in the text. Incidentally, this particular practice is linked to higher levels of reading comprehension (Wilkinson & Nelson, 2013). We want to highlight a few more instructional techniques that are particularly useful in differentiating process.

Read-alouds have a significant research base in support of them, and the practice enjoys widespread popularity (Layne, 2015). Interactive read-alouds, in which the teacher invites students to connect concepts with the author's vocabulary and use of academic language structures, are especially beneficial for English learners (Giroir, Grimaldo, Vaughn, & Roberts, 2015). The teacher might read a text aloud multiple times, each time focusing on a different purpose—to foster comprehension, to underline an aspect of the text that links to other knowledge bases, or to highlight aspects students can explore further through writing, debate, discussion, and investigation (Fisher & Frey, 2013).

Reading aloud is also acknowledged as a way of leveling the playing field for those who need more support in testing and instructional situations. Although some teachers maintain that reading a passage aloud gives some students an unfair edge, a major study by the National Assessment of Educational Progress (NAEP) refutes this. Reading passages aloud in testing significantly raised the scores of English learners and students with disabilities, but it did not impact the scores of native speakers without disabilities (Abedi, cited in Samuels, 2014). Although this study was conducted in a testing environment, there are implications for instruction as well. When the act of decoding messages from print interferes with a child's ability to learn concepts, reading information aloud to them is a useful way to provide access to the core curriculum. Teachers at the school where Doug and Nancy work often record themselves reading directions, texts, and test questions and post these on the school's LMS for any student to use.

Think-alouds, in which a teacher thinks aloud in real time with texts and during demonstrations, are a way to show students how experts actively monitor their own understanding, pose questions to themselves, resolve problems, and repair gaps in their knowledge. We have developed a think-aloud protocol for teacher use that demonstrates the range of metacognitive processes. Here's what it looks like when applied to the skill of resolving unknown words from a complex text:

1. *Name the strategy, skill, or task.* "Today I am going to show you how I resolve unfamiliar words."
2. *State the purpose of the strategy, skill, or task.* "Science texts often use new or unfamiliar terms that I have to try to figure out."
3. *Explain when the strategy or skill is used.* "When I run into a word or phrase I don't know, I remember that I have

three ways to solve it. The first way is to look inside of the word—at its parts. A second way is to look outside the word to see how it's used. Context clues can give me an idea about what the word means. If I can't solve it by looking inside or outside the word, I use a third problem-solving strategy, which is to use resources. I can check the glossary, ask a friend, or ask a teacher."

4. ***Use analogies to link prior knowledge to new learning.*** "It's like what I do when I am trying to find something I've lost. I begin by looking right around me, in the closest space. Next, I look a little further around me, and I turn all the way around. If I still can't find it, I ask for help."

5. ***Demonstrate how the skill, strategy, or task is completed.*** — A structural analysis of the term *sheltered*. "So one word I don't understand is *sheltered*. The first thing I'll do is take the word apart: *shelter-ed*. It's being used as an adjective, to describe an area—a *sheltered* area. I know that *shelter* is a noun that means a protected place with a roof. I'm guessing that a *sheltered area* is a place where there is a roof of some kind over an animal's head. I'll keep reading to see if that still makes sense and go back and check it later. I'll write the definition in the margin."

— A contextual analysis of the word *space*. "When I see the word *space*, the first thing I think about is outer space. But that definition doesn't make sense in this sentence or this article. I can't look inside the word, because there's nothing to break out. So I'll use my second problem-solving strategy, which is looking outside the word to see how it is used in context. [Rereads sentence] The author says here that 'the particular place where each animal lives in the forest is called a habitat.' I'm going to keep reading. [Rereads final sentence] There's *space* again. My guess is that the author is using *space* in a different way. The writer means that *space* is the amount of room an animal needs to live. I'm going to mark that, too."

6. ***Alert learners to errors to avoid.*** "I have to be careful not to forget to go back and check the words I was unsure of. If I still can't solve it, I will need to use my third problem-solving strategy, which is to use resources."

7. ***Assess the use of the skill.*** "Now I'll reread the sentences to make sure I am comfortable with the meanings."

By modeling *how* one goes about understanding what is being read or viewed, you give students tools for monitoring their own metacognitive processes. Think-alouds are especially useful when a student is able to face a complex text that is at his or her "frustration level" (Stahl, 2012). The experience of seeing a teacher find a way to make sense of challenging material and present a model to follow provides a bridge between the author's means of presentation and the content itself.

Guided instruction is an essential way to scaffold understanding. Modeling and thinking aloud create a cognitive path for students to follow, but the process of learning isn't complete until students assume cognitive responsibility and apply new knowledge on their own. However, few struggling students are ready to make an immediate jump to independent learning. They need to practice knowledge application in the company of their teacher. What's not helpful is a teacher who watches what students are doing and simply tells them if their attempts are correct or incorrect. What is helpful—and not just helpful but usually necessary—is guided instruction that will support and deepen understanding of the content. There are a number of ways that effective teachers do this, and these various approaches cluster into the following areas:

- *Robust questions* that probe students' thinking. These questions help students unearth their cognitive processes and invite them to consider alternatives. For example, when a teacher follows a student's comment with "Tell me more about that. Where did you find that information?" he is seeking and listening for evidence of the student's thinking and the sources she was using to inform herself.

- *Prompts* that facilitate cognitive and metacognitive behavior. Prompts provide students with hints that they can use to make connections and get back on track. They also provide students an opportunity to reflect on their thinking and revise their responses. For example, when Maria Sanchez responded to a student with "Is your answer consistent with the author's message? I'm thinking about the way that the author explained forces of nature and the video we watched a few days ago," she was providing prompts for the student to rethink her answer.

- *Cues* that shift learners' attention to information or ideas that they have missed. Cues can be verbal, visual, gestural, or positional (the location or orientation of an object), but they always point the learner to something he or she missed without directly telling the student what that is. For example, when Jeff Sheldon said to a student, "Let's take another look at the figure on page 112. The columns might help more than the rows," he was shifting the learner's attention to a specific source without revealing the answer.

Guided instruction is a critical instructional practice to master precisely because too frequently, struggling students' uncertain or partial answers are misunderstood as a lack of knowledge. Often, these students lack just a particular piece of scaffolding that will allow them to make missing connections. Choosing to use guided instruction rather than supply answers to struggling students is another way we can communicate high expectations.

Leveled questions provide a way to scaffold critical thinking. As students advance through the grades, those who struggle to understand the texts used to build content knowledge are at risk for falling further behind with each passing year (Chall & Jacobs, 2003). Given the importance of text comprehension as a conduit for content knowledge, it is surprising how little attention is given to how the hardest-to-teach students access text. Evidence of this relative inattention is the widespread practice of "one and done" readings, especially outside the reading block. Consider how often you've followed (or witnessed) this process: (1) asked the class to read a passage silently; (2) asked some questions about the reading; (3) called on the same handful of students who always seem to answer; and then (4) moved on to a new lesson segment. Chances are, many of the students who sat quietly throughout the question-and-answer period were unwilling or unable to share that they didn't understand what they had read.

At some point in their careers, many educators realize that the "one and done" reading model isn't a very good way to ensure text comprehension. A lot of them then proceed to overcorrect, frontloading so much textual information before a reading assignment that there isn't much left for students to find themselves. Mind you, frontloading is beneficial practice when students possess a significant knowledge gap and need explanation in advance of the reading to help them contextualize (Echevarría et al., 2017). However, without careful attention to classroom discourse before and after the reading, frontloading won't help students develop the kind of understanding we aim for. The types of questions teachers ask about what students read, and the order in which we ask these questions, can significantly boost deep comprehension of the text (Fisher & Frey, 2014).

Struggling readers in particular benefit from *leveled questions* that will move them from literal to structural understandings of the text, building a strong foundation for the critical and inferential thinking that is indicative of deep comprehension. We categorize these questions as four stages of text-based discussion and investigation (Fisher & Frey, 2013):

1. *What does the text say?* (Literal-level questions about key details and general understandings)

2. *How does the text work?* (Structure-level questions about vocabulary, text organization, and the author's craft)
3. *What does the text mean?* (Inferential-level questions that challenge students to interpret, use reasoning, and form opinions within and across texts)
4. *What does the text inspire you to do?* (Investigations, research, debates, writing, Socratic seminars)

The struggling readers in your classroom, regardless of the reason they may struggle, are capable of engaging in the critical analysis of a text, but to do so, they must first have a good handle on what the text says and how the text works. Unfortunately, in "one and done" readings, the first two stages are often given short shrift, while the more interesting inferential levels are pushed on students too soon. Our experience has been that when we take the time to build students' knowledge of what the text says and how it works through dialogic teaching, the struggling readers gain the traction they need. Effective teachers don't just ask the question—they also press for evidence. Asking, "Where did you find that information? Can everyone look?" is an easy way to guide all the readers in the class back into the text ("rereading") and help them develop their comprehension.

Fifth grade social studies students in Noura Rahal's class were engaged in a geography unit of study framed by the essential question "How do the extremes of geography, climate, and natural resources affect the way people live and work?" As part of their investigation, they would be reading excerpts from Steve Jenkins's nonfiction picture book, *The Top of the World: Climbing Mount Everest.* Ms. Rahal began the lesson by revisiting the essential question, establishing the purpose for the lesson, and locating Mount Everest on a map of the world. She read aloud the first paragraph, which established some factual information about the mountain, including its height and the fact that it was unknown to the outside world until about 200 years ago. Then

Ms. Rahal asked her students to read the next four paragraphs silently (she had recorded her own voice reading it so that two students who read significantly below grade level could follow along using headphones).

After the reading, Ms. Rahal led the class through a series of questions she had prepared in advance (see Figure 3.2), skipping a question here and there when it had already been covered in the discussion. For example, she didn't ask the literal-level question about the Sherpas because it had already come up for discussion. However, she did end up spending more time exploring the connection between the phrases *low oxygen* and *thin air* when she posed an inferential-level question related to the latter. "It wasn't until I said *thin air* that I realized that many of them didn't really know what that term meant," she said. The class spent about 20 minutes discussing this text, which would provide the structure for the remainder of the lesson. "I've learned that if I spend a little more time with a reading like this, I can use it to spur inquiry and investigation," she said. She posed the four investigation questions for students to choose from, and for the next 30 minutes students worked in small, self-selected groups to locate information. They reconvened as a class for the last 10 minutes of the period, sharing information about what they had learned thus far. "I get some great insight into who needs what, based on what they have been able to unearth," Ms. Rahal explained. "The next day's lesson is often in part an extension of what they want to know next."

Differentiate products

The products that students create provide teachers with a means for assessing progress toward learning goals. However, these goals are likely to vary somewhat among the students in the class, who may be working at different paces, via different activities, and with different sets of supports. As important as it is to set individual goals with students, it is equally important that the products

FIGURE 3.2

Leveled Questions for *The Top of the World: Climbing Mount Everest*

Question Type	Examples
What does the text say? (Literal level)	• How high is Mount Everest? • What extremes are encountered on and near Mount Everest? • Who are the Sherpas? • What are the effects of low oxygen on humans? • What is another term the author uses to describe having too little oxygen?
How does the text work? (Structural level)	• How does the writer help you to understand what the terms *acclimate* and *summit* mean? • What is the relationship between altitude and oxygen levels? • The writer says, "If you ever want to climb it, here are a few things to think about." What are the facts he wants you to consider? • How does the heading "Home Away from Home" link to the information about base camps, even though the writer never repeats the phrase? • How would you describe the writer's opinion about the mountain? What words and phrases does he use that support your answer?
What does the text mean? (Inferential level)	• Why is it about the Sherpas' life that makes it possible for them to be on the mountain, considering that we've already been told that thin air can be fatal? • Are Sherpas key to a successful climb? • What kind of preparation would a climber need to ascend the mountain?
What does the text inspire you to do? (Investigation)	• In this excerpt, the author doesn't explain why the journey down the mountain can be the most dangerous part of the trip. How can you investigate this statement further? • How do the other highest mountains on Earth compare to Everest in terms of climate and how people live? • What factors contributed to unsuccessful climbs? • How do Sherpas earn a living when it is not climbing season?

they create are aligned with these goals. In other words, it's not fair to expect students who possess a wide range of readiness levels, interests, and preferred ways of learning to achieve and demonstrate mastery in the same way via the same assignment.

Many struggling students are labeled as such simply because their teachers ask them to "show what they know" in a format that's a mismatch for their abilities. We're not suggesting that students have carte blanche or free rein, but rather that teachers should consider that there are many ways for students to demonstrate their learning. Time and time again, we have encountered students who won't even try because they believe that they "can't write" or are terrified at the idea of having to give a speech or who freeze up at the sight of a test.

This is not to say that you need to create 30 different product assignments for a class of 30 students, but when you are planning how you monitor and assess students' learning, be mindful of how differentiation based on student interest and learning profile might give you a more accurate picture. We'll examine ways to do that now.

Offering product choice means allowing the students themselves to decide how they will show you what they are learning. It can be a particularly powerful force for those who struggle. The research testifies to choice's significant role in motivation, and motivation has long been acknowledged as a key element of learning (see Guthrie & Wigfield, 2000). In fact, a study of more than 300 high school juniors and seniors demonstrated that motivation was as predictive of achievement in a subject as intelligence (Steinmayr & Spinath, 2009). Unfortunately, the link between motivation and achievement is often overlooked in the classroom. Think of how many times you've heard poor performance explained with a shrug and the comment that the student "just isn't motivated." We believe that everyone is motivated by something; as teachers, we struggle to find the right motivators to reach our students. Providing choice through open-ended tasks is an effective way to address both performance and motivation issues.

For example, in the English classrooms at Doug and Nancy's high school, teachers read target texts with students as a whole class and allow student choice for related reading. Both the target text and the student selections are organized according to the schoolwide essential question. To address the essential question "What is race, and does it matter?" an 11th grade English teacher assigned Lorraine Hansberry's *A Raisin in the Sun* as the in-class target text. However, students also selected another text from a list of fiction and nonfiction options to read independently and discuss. Four students chose to read the graphic novel *American Born Chinese,* by Gene Luen Yang. They met several times a week as they read the book, with the essential question serving as the guideline for their discussions. After making some decisions about the pacing of the discussions, the group chose to focus on the parallels between *A Raisin in the Sun* and *American Born Chinese* and the ways in which the two genres (a play and a graphic novel) dictated the story. One student (a chronic underachiever) later wrote the following in an essay addressing the essential question "What is race, and does it matter?":

> The characters of Jin Wang and Beneatha Younger had very different experiences, but would probably answer this question the same way. Yes, race does matter. Each tried to overcome, even deny, their race, but in the end their racial and culture experiences made them who they are. The metaphor of the Monkey King in *American Born Chinese* could be a lesson to both: the path to self-awareness begins with self-acceptance. Only when you understand who you are can you then decide who you will become.

The insight this student brought to the work was surprising, as he had gained a reputation for putting forth minimal effort. As we watched him develop as a learner that year, we saw a transformation in his identity as well. His teacher discovered that his need for choice was a tool she could use to foster his active participation in his own learning.

Let's look at a few ways that differentiating products helps to increase student motivation.

When younger children are offered choice, they get to explore their interests. Because they are interested, they are mentally engaged, and thus more likely to develop the skills and stamina of accomplished readers and writers. In Hilda Lopez's 4th grade classroom, shelves are lined with bins containing a variety of books organized by topic. Importantly, each bin includes texts representing a range of reading levels. "I want them to get experience at finding the right book for them," Ms. Lopez explained, "and not rely on me to match them by reading level. If they want to read about tornados, or amphibians, or female characters in historical fiction, I've got lots of books for them to select from." Ms. Lopez not only provides choice according to student interest but also teaches students *how* to make good choices. One way she does this is by displaying a "How to Select a Book" poster in the classroom. It prompts students to consider factors such as how interesting the title is, the back cover information, whether the book is by an author they know and like, whether it's a book in a series they're reading, and whether it was recommended by a friend or teacher.

Once students have selected a book, Ms. Lopez advises them to read the first chapter to gauge their interest and see if it's really suitable for them. Children who are unsure about whether to continue with a title after doing so meet with Ms. Lopez to discuss other possible strategies for continuing successfully (e.g., talk to someone else who has read it; search an online retailer's website to read a synopsis and review; check to see if there is an audio recording available). In some cases, students go back to the bin and select another book that is a better fit. "Everyone has the right to abandon a book," said Ms. Lopez. "I know I do it. But I want them to know why they are doing so and make a plan for what comes next. Nothing is worse than a child who decides reading is not for them simply because they never found the right books."

Ms. Lopez differentiates product assignments in all content areas, providing her students with several options for demonstrating their understanding. For instance, after researching a science topic and gathering information, she allows students to use the information to prepare a short film, brochure, PowerPoint presentation, e-book, or slide show and then present their product to the class. However, she knows that these sound approaches to differentiated instruction are not sufficient for building academic language skills for her students. To further accelerate academic language proficiency, she provides language instruction throughout the day, integrating it into her science, social studies, mathematics, and arts instruction.

Open-ended projects, such as independent studies and "Genius Hour" explorations, are more good ways to incorporate product differentiation and boost motivation. Ivan Amante, a high school English teacher, believes that work done outside school should be interesting and should require students to work with at least one other person. He is most interested in independent projects that require students to interact with their families. He is *least* interested in independent projects that encourage students to sit in their bedrooms by themselves. This has led him to embrace the practice of offering students a choice of a range of project options. While working on a unit on the Middle Ages, some students opted to interview an elder family member on how the concept of childhood has changed over his or her lifetime. Students had been exploring how, in the Middle Ages, children were basically seen as "little adults." They had read informational text about marriage laws of the time and were shocked to find out that girls often married at age 12 and boys at 14. This particular product option had them compare their older family members' thoughts on evolution of "childhood" with what they had learned about life in the Middle Ages. Mr. Amante found this independent project to be particularly successful for the English learners in his classes because they were permitted to complete the assignment in their home language. Other students worked together outside school to film an iMovie using the school's digital camera. Inspired by their readings of *Catherine, Called Birdy* and *Matilda Bone,* they created a day-in-the-life comparison of a servant girl and the daughter of a lord. Jen, a student with a significant disability, used her augmentative communication device to perform her lines in the video. Tina Duong, the special education teacher, programmed the device in advance for Jen and her friends. Julian made plans to include this short iMovie on the class's website.

As another example, Chavez Middle School schedules a daily advisory period, which offers a range of classes students can sign up for based on their interest in various topics. Some of the recent advisory class topics have included the sinking of the *Titanic*, graphic novels, and careers in human services. Each class runs for three weeks, after which students pick a new class with a new topic. Some students make different choices each term; others choose whatever class Mary Arnold is teaching, regardless of the topic. Ms. Arnold believes that these interest groups allow students to experience the richness of a curriculum, make choices about what they want to learn, and demonstrate their learning in multiple ways. For example, some students choose to write, others create presentations, and still others engage in debates based on what they have learned. She knows that the time she spends in advisory allows her to get to know students well.

More recently, Chavez Middle School has redesigned its bell schedule to include a weekly Genius Hour in which students undertake independent projects of their own design. The school developed a bank of essential questions to drive student projects, then created a menu of experts on staff to provide advice and guidance. For example, one math teacher offered his services for any student looking for help with anime software. One student focusing on the essential question "How does where you live affect how you live?" conducted research comparing and contrasting his family's experiences living in Somalia and in the United States. After interviewing family members and researching facts about both countries, he met with the math teacher during weekly Genius Hour sessions to storyboard his script, then turn it into a short animated film. The student presented the film as a gift to his family, who were delighted to see their words and insights captured in cartoon form.

Genius Hour is being adopted by an increasing number of schools to foster creativity and raise students' sense of autonomy and agency in what they learn about. Interestingly, educators working in schools with a Genius Hour report higher levels of school library circulation and usage, stronger relationships between students and teachers, and positive reports from parents, students, and teachers. "It's really awakened all of us on staff to the many interests our students have," said Ms. Arnold. "We accomplished lots of good things over the years with our advisory period studies, but the topics were always selected by the teachers. In moving to Genius Hour, we've put our students in the driver's seat to investigate their passions and unlock their own creativity," she continued. "We always talk about inspiring students with the content we teach, but if we don't give them an outlet and the supports they need to explore, any inspiration will fade."

Use Accommodations and Modifications as Needed

Although the language used to talk about the kind of adaptive practices that help students with disabilities access the curriculum is specialized, the underlying principles align with differentiation. Special education uses the terms *accommodation* and *modification* to describe the ways students with disabilities and IEPs gain access to curriculum, both through services and supports.* Accommodations are changes to how a student gains information and demonstrates mastery—the inputs and outputs, if you will. Modifications are more significant, as they are changes to what is being learned. In other words, modifications refer to extensive alterations of curriculum so that it focuses on a much smaller aspect of the content. Remember, both accommodations and modifications can be viewed through the lens of content, process, and product.

Accommodations, which are employed with the majority of students with disabilities, change how the content is presented and how students are called on to engage with it and demonstrate their knowledge.

- *Content accommodations* include chunking concepts into smaller segments and providing additional time and practice.
- *Process accommodations* include changing the setting, providing a peer note taker, using a prerecorded reading, or furnishing an alternate format of a text to a student with a print-processing disability.
- *Product accommodations* include providing alternate assignments, using speech recognition software to compose, and furnishing visual organizers to support planning.

This isn't an exhaustive list, but it illustrates a key point: Accommodations do not significantly alter *what* a student is learning, and a student receiving accommodations should be working toward meeting district and state requirements for graduation. Characteristically, accommodations do not alter a task's complexity, but they may make a task less difficult. Note that difficulty and complexity are not the same thing; the latter

---

* Just because a student has a disability or receives special education services does not automatically mean that he or she needs every kind of adaptation available. We like to keep "OASAN" in mind: *Only As Special As Necessary.*

is a measure of student effort; the former is a feature of the task itself. To illustrate, the task of memorizing the names of all the world capitals is difficult, but it isn't complex; it's really just a low-level recall task. Understanding that capital cities are often located in areas that are conducive to protection, commerce, and transportation may or may not be a difficult task, depending on the student who undertakes it, but it's certainly a more complex task than recall. Perhaps that's why the latter, but not the former, appears in social studies standards.

Modifications, on the other hand, are designed and employed for students with more significant disabilities that impact their learning. Modifications change what students are expected to learn and thus affect both a task's difficulty and its complexity.

- *Content modifications* include identifying essential content that focuses on partial knowledge of the topic and using specialized or alternate curricular materials in place of standard course textbooks.
- *Process modifications* include providing reading material at the student's independent level, which is significantly below same-age peers; using visuals in place of text to convey ideas; and simplifying vocabulary and concepts to meet the student's level of understanding.
- *Product modifications* include grading modifications based on a student's individual progress rather than standard success criteria and using alternate assessment instruments to gauge progress.

Students who receive modifications often exit high school with a certificate of completion rather than a standard diploma. Their general education experiences are customized—based on the decisions the IEP team has reached about the student's learning. The general and special educators on the student's team work in tandem to create a cohesive and individualized course of learning. While students using modified curriculum represent only a very small portion of the U.S. school population (estimated to be 1 to 3 percent of the overall number of students with IEPs), they benefit enormously from it, and their presence in classrooms benefits their peers as well. Consider that many common classroom technologies that now support the learning of all have their roots in supporting people with disabilities, including the QWERTY keyboard on your computer, the speech recognition software on your smartphone, and the e-mail program you use, which was developed as a way for people who are deaf to communicate.

• • •

Students deserve access to high-quality curriculum and instruction. Failure to provide this access prevents students from achieving and likely contributes to their negative self-talk and frustration with school. In sum, our expectations for high-quality instruction are fairly simple. Classrooms should be purpose-driven, and the purpose for learning should be communicated to students. Learners should be engaged in tasks that allow them to consolidate their understanding in the presence of their peers. Rich academic language should permeate the environment and errors should be addressed, but students should not be simply told answers. Further, students should be expected to demonstrate their learning individually in different formats, and that is a topic we will address further in the next chapter.

Assessment to Inform Instruction

Alex Uribe sits at his desk after school, reviewing slips of paper on which his students have written their responses to the exit question of the day, "How are the common forms of government (monarchy, democracy, republic, dictatorship) different?" As Mr. Uribe reviews his students' work, he notices that they have consistently used the key vocabulary from the unit and show a strong understanding of the essential characteristics of these four forms of government. He makes a note to congratulate his students on the understanding they're developing. They are well prepared for the projects they'll be taking on in the next stage of the unit and on track to ace the summative assessment at the unit's end.

As he continues his review of the exit card responses, Mr. Uribe notices that three students did not correctly describe a republic. He makes a note to talk with these students about their thinking related to republics, and he marks a page in the textbook that he will have them reread to solidify their understanding. He also notes that nearly all of his students indicated that monarchies are governed by kings—an assumption he'll need to challenge. Mr. Uribe opens his laptop to find current information about Queen Elizabeth II of England. Mr. Uribe notes to himself that assuming monarchies are governed by kings isn't a major misunderstanding and might be a simple pronoun issue, but he wants to ensure that his students understand that absolute primogeniture (succession to the throne by the first-born male) is not practiced in many modern monarchies. On the official website of the British monarchy, he flags a section related to "The Queen's Day," which will also help his students understand the differences between a modern ruler and those they have read about in their textbook.

Turning back to the exit cards, he sees that Araceli wrote, "I very confused. Democracy is voting, like USA. Dictatorship is Cuba. But what it is?" Mr. Uribe puts Araceli's paper aside, knowing that he needs to make time the following day to meet with her while the other students engage in a collaborative task. He locates a compare/contrast graphic organizer to use in this one-on-one discussion.

In this scenario, we see how Mr. Uribe uses the data generated by a quick assessment to guide his instruction and help his students understand the social studies curriculum (and the world) a little better. We have talked about the hallmarks of an effective teacher, and this is another of them: looking at student work and noticing areas where additional instruction is necessary. There are a number of ways to collect this assessment information, but data collection is only half of the equation, and on its own, it changes nothing. The combination of checking for understanding and then taking action on the data is what allows teachers to use assessment to inform instruction and make adjustments in the classroom. The process works both to keep students on track and to get struggling students on track and position them for future success.

Assessment is the driver for instruction; deploying it in this manner is even more critical for students who are not currently making expected progress. We must closely monitor these students in order to refine our instructional approaches in a way that will accelerate their progress. Although there are resources available that explore formal diagnostic assessments in great detail, these are beyond the scope of our book. What we are concerned with here are the many ways teachers can use regular checks for understanding to monitor and then foster student learning, paying particular attention, of course, to students who struggle. Here are the actions we recommend:

- Allocate unequal resources for unequal needs.
- Learn and apply assessment principles for hard-to-teach students.
- Use speaking and listening to check for understanding.
- Use writing to check for understanding.
- Use projects and portfolios to check for understanding.
- Foster goal setting.
- Use assessment data to design interventions.

Allocate Unequal Resources for Unequal Needs

We do not subscribe to the idea that fairness means providing everyone in the classroom with the same type of instruction on the same schedule. The fact is, some students need more instructional attention at a given moment than others, and in our minds, fairness requires that we provide what is needed to those who need it.

Fair—and effective—teachers notice when a student isn't making progress and take action to get that student back on track. They notice where students are ready to extend their thinking and provide the path forward. For some teachers, perhaps, this noticing is instinctual; for the rest of us, it's a deliberate, intentional undertaking. It requires systematic checks for understanding using a variety of techniques to gauge the process of individuals and groups, followed by strategic error analysis to determine where the learning needs are and how best to address them.

Mr. Uribe's analysis of the exit slips in his social studies class informed his plans for the next day. He was able to identify where to focus his instructional resources: which students needed his direct support and what that support would be. Critically, he formatted his instruction to provide this support without neglecting or slowing down students who were ready to move on. He arranged for the students who performed well on the assessment to keep moving forward through meaningful collaborative learning—working with their peers, using academic language, agreeing and disagreeing about ideas and information, and producing excellent work. His plans provided them with a forum for sharing their thinking and critically examining their own understandings. It's important to note that when it comes to meeting student needs, the targeted support aspect of instruction informed by assessment works both ways. Mr. Uribe could easily meet with individuals or small groups of students who are thriving to ask questions or tailor assignments to push their thinking to new heights.

Structuring a classroom to combine large-group, small-group, and one-on-one instruction is a great way to ensure fair allocation of instructional resources. While many or even most students are engaged in collaborative learning with their peers, the teacher can meet with specific students who would benefit from the focused attention. Fourth grade teacher Emma Rodriguez embraces this approach. Her students work collaboratively on a daily basis, and she intentionally forms and re-forms the work groups to ensure a diverse mix of strengths and needs in each. As the groups work, Ms. Rodriguez asks some students to meet with her, leaving their group temporarily. Often these small-group, needs-based lessons are designed to address the gaps in students' understanding. But Ms. Rodriguez also uses this process to meet with students who have demonstrated mastery so that she can ensure that they understand the content at a deeper level. As she says, "I meet with the highest-performing students on a regular basis, but certainly not daily. Other students, I meet with for instruction daily or, for some, multiple times a day." In this way, the support she provides students is aligned with their needs. Some students need more, right now, than others. Importantly, that can change from unit to unit or week to week. Keeping track of student needs, and then adjusting instructional arrangements to meet those needs, is an assumption we make about effective classroom instruction.

Learn and Apply Assessment Principles for Hard-to-Teach Students

Assessment is often perceived as something that happens after the learning has occurred. In truth, it begins before students arrive on the first day of school, and it is woven, formally and informally, throughout individual lessons and units of instruction. Every time a teacher checks for understanding, that teacher gathers data on student progress toward content mastery, which can inform his or her next set of instructional decisions. Using assessment data formatively is beneficial for all students, but it's critical for students who are not making expected progress.

Students who struggle with learning and language have more intensive assessment needs than their classmates. Put simply, you can't build effective instruction for them based on the results of periodic quizzes and data from summative exams. Here are the formative principles that should guide your approach.

Assess frequently

Exit slips, observations, skills checklists, and other checks for understanding should be collected frequently, and those of struggling students should be prioritized for analysis. Secondary teachers may find themselves with 180 exit slips on a single day, so this prioritization is important. Keep a list of students who need more frequent checks, and set a reminder on your digital calendar to look at the work they completed that day. Keep anecdotal notes of their progress and the reteaching points you've identified and addressed so you can chart trends across the semester or school year.

Assess language learning, not just content learning

The oral and written academic language used in the classroom is key to understanding concepts; for this reason, assessing language along with content knowledge will yield more insight into struggling students' status and needs in regard to both. In a study of struggling middle school students, Espin, Shin, and Busch (2005) found that struggling students' ability to match social studies terms to definitions was an efficient and valid curriculum-based measure of those students' progress in social studies. Another curriculum-linked way to check in on language is to ask a student to give you a spoken summary of a lesson. By listening for the ways she constructs sentences and organizes ideas, you can determine whether she needs further instruction related to syntax, grammar, and content. Still another method for getting this kind of information is to take a 100- to 200-word summary passage in a textbook and remove every fifth word. Ask the students to complete the passage, and note who is having difficulty with grammar and syntax. These cloze assessments (Taylor, 1953) provide an efficient assessment of language and content knowledge. You can find free cloze test generators online. Some allow you to delete words based on word type as well as a fixed interval.

Provide assessment accommodations to increase validity

Validity is a concern in any assessment. Be mindful of confounding characteristics that can skew your data. Of course, a student who arrives at school fatigued and without breakfast is probably going to perform less well on an assessment given that day, but factors such as language development, stamina, and disability can also interfere with performance. Be prepared to use assessment adaptations that will help neutralize these factors and support more valid results, including reducing the range of questions, varying the testing time, adjusting the difficulty level, changing the final product, and adjusting the expected means of participation. Figure 4.1 provides a detailed table of these adaptations.

FIGURE 4.1
Assessment Adaptations

Adaptation Type	Process
Range	Adapt the number of items the student is expected to complete, such as only the odd or even numbers, only the first 10 items from a 15-item list, or only the first 2 steps of a 4-step assessment.
Time	Adapt the amount of time the student has to complete the assessment by providing more processing time, breaking tasks into smaller chunks, or extending the time line for completion.
Level of support	Adapt the amount of scaffolding provided to students during the assessment by asking an aide, peer, or parent volunteer to explain the task, read the task aloud, or translate the task.
Difficulty	Adapt the skill level, type of problem or task, and the process for how a student can access or approach the task, such as allowing use of a calculator, a dictionary, or spell check.
Product	Adapt the type of response the student is allowed to make, such as a verbal response instead of a written one, an illustration instead of a verbal response, or a hands-on demonstration rather than a traditional test response.
Participation	Adapt the degree of active involvement expected of the student by encouraging individual self-assessment, providing assistance in creating rubrics, or permitting cooperative group assessments.

Source: From *Making Content Comprehensible for English Learners: The SIOP® Model* (5th ed.) (p. 239) by J. Echevarría, M. E. Vogt, & D. Short, 2017. Boston: Allyn & Bacon. Copyright 2017 by Allyn & Bacon. Adapted with permission.

Use assessment results to guide needs-based instruction

The point of checking for understanding is to organize needs-based instruction. In the scenario at the beginning of this chapter, Mr. Uribe used his review of exit card responses to determine how he should adjust his instructional plans for the following day. Cataloging group error trends is useful for determining when the entire class needs reteaching, as opposed to when a select group of students need further instruction. Note that reteaching should be anticipated as a regular and necessary part of practice. Setting aside time each week for small-group reteaching ensures your ability to provide the direct, additional support that hard-to-teach students require.

Consult with specialist colleagues on assessment results

Be sure to meet regularly with inclusion support specialists, English language development coaches, Title I teachers, or any other specialist colleagues who support the struggling learners you teach to consult about student progress, trends, and when it is time to fade scaffolds. More often than not, these specialists will work directly with individual students on occasion, but they don't spend nearly as much time with them as you, the classroom teacher, do. By coordinating services and sharing assessment results, you and specialist staff can ensure that every student is experiencing a coherent educational program.

English learners benefit from many of the same assessment practices as English-proficient students, but the simple fact of the language barrier makes the work of getting a valid picture of understanding that much more complicated. Just imagine if you had to travel to another country and take a class on a topic you know little about—calculus, for example, or computer programming or astronomy. Would you appear to have learning problems? Would you be motivated to listen closely throughout a 20-, 45-, or 60-minute lecture given in a language you have just a rudimentary facility with if you had little opportunity to clarify what is being said and what is expected from you as a learner? The effort it takes to concentrate in another language should not be underestimated, and it must be factored in during assessments. Sometimes we are quick to attribute learning difficulties to the students when, in fact, they simply have not had sufficient opportunity to learn in the ways we advocate for in this book, or the assessment isn't set up to reveal the student's learning rather than his or her English proficiency. Figure 4.2 lists some important questions to consider when preparing assessments for English learners.

FIGURE 4.2
Considerations for Assessing English Learners

1. Are the instructions for completing the task clear?

2. Are you giving ample time for the student to complete the task?

3. Are you familiar enough with the student's English proficiency level to recognize the progress the student is making, however incremental?

4. Is the language demand of the assessment too high for the student's English proficiency level?

5. Are you repeating the directions, as needed? Can the student explain to you what you want him or her to do on the assessment?

6. Does the student need the instructions translated into his or her home language?

7. Have you pretaught the vocabulary of the task you're assessing the student on?

Source: Echevarría et al., 2015.

Use Speaking and Listening to Check for Understanding

Asking and answering questions in class is a fundamental way that teachers check for content understanding. It has the added benefit of being an excellent source of language proficiency information for English learners (Short & Echevarría, 2016) as well students who need to work on academic vocabulary. In addition to asking students to listen to and respond to questions posed, teachers can also invite students to retell or explain information that they have read or heard. As Hattie (2009) noted, classroom discussions have a significant impact on students' learning. As students engage in content discussion, teachers can identify errors and misconceptions and address them in real time. Importantly, speaking and listening also allow students to clarify their own understanding. We cannot count the number of students who have told us, "I didn't know what I thought until I had to say it out loud."

Of course, using oral language to check for understanding presents some practical challenges. It's not enough to ask questions that you already know the answer to—the ones that require students to "guess what's in the teacher's head." Frankly, some students don't care, while others don't want to risk answering incorrectly. To get a sense of what students really know and understand, it's essential to include questions that have no clear answer. You want to prompt students to expand upon their own thinking, elaborate on their own ideas, and give you a window into their comprehension. Another challenge of whole-class question-and-answer periods is that there isn't enough time for every student in the class to retell what they have learned or respond to the questions necessary to gauge their comprehension. For this reason, a lot of the discussion needs to occur between partners and in small groups of students—setups that give students time to practice and develop both discussion skill and content understanding and require the teacher to move around the room, listening to different students and responding to their correct and incorrect answers.

Use digital tools

Technology allows teachers to gather oral responses from many students at once and to play them back later for thorough analysis. For example, the 6th grade students in Brad Weinberg's class read *Chasing Cheetahs: The Race to Save Africa's Fastest Cats* by Sy Montgomery and Nic Bishop. As one of their learning stations for the day, students used their tablets and an app called Aurasma to record a response to a part of the book that resonated with them. Then they used the tablet camera to take a picture the particular passage—a "trigger image" that, when scanned, would play their recorded response. For example, Ricardo chose page 13 and recorded these comments:

> The cheetahs are disappearing from the world because their environments are being destroyed. There used to be about 100,000 and now there are just 10,000. Lots of people are involved with trying to save them. This page really was important because it shows how hard it is for this to happen. Scientists have a lot of questions and still have a lot of work to do to figure out things. I thought it was interesting that some people think that the cheetahs are a problem and they want them gone. The author says that they have to get people to change their beliefs.

Generally, tablets will have a voice recorder function to capture student retellings even without specific apps. The 1st grade students in Alex Aguilar's class recorded one another retelling the content from a shared reading that their teacher had done. As part of a unit of study on friendship, Mr. Aguilar read aloud an article about a kidney transplant. The students worked in pairs to record their retellings, with one person holding the tablet and the other speaking. Yareli said, "Transplant means to give somebody something from inside your body, like a kidney, so that they can stay alive. This guy helped his friend because his kidney didn't work and he was very sick." Mr. Aguilar has a number of English learners in his class, and he usually pairs English learners with fluent English speakers so the English speakers can help their classmates in expressing their ideas. At other times, he pairs a beginning English learner with a more fluent English learner and encourages them to use their home language as needed to more accurately express comprehension of the content.

Kindergarten teacher Kendra Richards uses the Tell About This app (www.tellaboutapp.com) to create customized "Tell Abouts" linked to their social studies and science units of study. During a unit on weather, Ms. Richards used prompts already in the program, as well as some she designed. Her students saw photographs of different weather conditions paired with a voiced prompt asking them to tell about what was occurring in the photo. For instance, one photograph in the program showed a child playing in the snow, paired with the prompt "How would you have fun in the snow?" A simple interface allows the child to record a voice response to the prompt. Ms. Richards uses the students' "Tell Abouts" to foster further discussion during their science circles, as when she paired a photograph of storm clouds with the prompt "How do you get ready to go outside when the sky looks like this?" She played several "Tell About" responses, listing the items and processes the children mentioned. She then led students in a List-Group-Label strategy (Taba, 1967), guiding them as they grouped items into categories and then labeled the categories they created. "I like using the Tell Abouts because I get to listen closely to their ideas. But what I really like is using them to promote listening skills. They seem to listen more attentively to one another when it's a recording. They'll sometimes ask me to play the recording again because they realized they missed something. I get to gauge how they're progressing, and what content I might need to reteach," said Ms. Richards.

Speech therapist Lisa Cervantes uses a similar program called Expressive Builder (http://mobile-educationstore.com/apps/narrative-skills/language-builder-for-ipad-2) with some of the students she sees in Ms. Richards's classroom. Using prompts similar to those designed by the teacher for Tell About This, Ms. Cervantes is able to construct digital language frames to support their answers. "Some of them need more support with sentence ideation and formation," she said. "But I'm not always there to provide that. The app allows Ms. Richards to e-mail me their voice recordings so I can analyze them before the next session. I get lots more authentic information about how they're doing in the classroom, which helps me tailor my therapy to align with their needs," she said.

Conduct group checks for understanding

Another way around the time requirements of using speaking and listening to check for understanding is to provide an inclusive response opportunity. Audience response has been around for a long time. For example, students can be asked to put their thumbs up if they agree and thumbs down if they disagree with a statement or question. They can hold up cards with a word written on them (e.g., yes/no, true/false) to represent their thinking.

Socrative (www.socrative.com) is a system that allows for audience responses to be gathered electronically, using mobile phones, tablets, or computers. The system also organizes responses so that teachers can determine who still needs instruction and who seems to understand the content. The formats include multiple choice, true/false, short answer, and so on.

The students in Dalia Lopez's 3rd grade class were involved in a unit of study related to inventors, focusing on the question "What are the common characteristics of inventors?" As part of their investigation, they read *Mr. Ferris and His Wheel* by Kathryn Gibbs Davis and Gilbert Ford. Ms. Lopez often uses the race format in Socrative, allowing students to work in teams to see which group can be the first to answer all of the questions correctly. Ms. Lopez asks a range of literal, structural, and inferential questions (see Fisher, Frey, Anderson, & Thayre, 2015) that require students to draw on evidence from the text. Here's a sample:

- Place these inventions in chronological order: Eiffel Tower, Ferris wheel, skyscraper.

- What does *outshine* mean? How did the author help you figure out that word?
- What was the inspiration for the world's first skyscraper?
- How was the national contest for the location of the World's Fair announced? Why would it be announced that way?
- Why did the judges for the Chicago World's Fair vote no on drawings of towers?

The students worked feverishly, talking with each other before responding on their tablets. Ms. Lopez listened in on these student conversations, periodically checking her tablet to determine which questions groups were mastering and which they were not. She took note of their understanding so that she could reread parts of the text again.

Fifth grade teacher Demetrius Bryant uses GoSoapBox (www.gosoapbox.com), a web-based clicker app, to spark discussion in his classroom. In preparation for Earth Day, he developed a science lesson in which students read a number of books and informational articles about environmental protection issues. One book, *When Rivers Burned: The Earth Day Story,* described events leading up to the first Earth Day in 1970. Mr. Bryant posed discussion questions about DDT, the fire that raged in the polluted Cuyahoga River, environmentalist Gaylord Nelson, and other topics and notable figures. Students in Mr. Bryant's class responded to his posted questions using the app, which gathered their responses in a central display. "When I pose a question, I always ask them to convince their table partners about the accuracy or reasonableness of their response before opening it to the entire group," he explained. "I never reveal an answer or my opinion about something until they've had time to process this as a group." A feature he especially appreciates is a "confusion barometer" that allows students to indicate they need more information. "When I asked them to identify evidence of progress since 1970, they were able to give lots of examples," said Mr. Bryant. "But when I asked about evidence that some environmental problems are worse than ever, like 19 kids hit that confusion barometer. I spent time taking them back through some other readings we had discussed last week, like the drought in the western United States and the continued loss of amphibians. I'm not sure that I would have done that if I hadn't given them a way to signal that they weren't with me," he said. "I've noticed that it's improved my teaching practice, too." He added, "It's reminding me that I need to prompt that metacognitive thinking, where they have to self-assess."

Use Writing to Check for Understanding

Students' written responses have long been used as a source of assessment data. Writing is a record of thinking, and writing provides a glimpse inside a student's brain to see what and how that student understands. Like speaking, writing allows students to clarify their own understanding. Writing prompts also reduce the pressure that some students feel to respond publicly (and, potentially, to be judged). One challenge with using writing to check for understanding is the amount of time it generally requires. Having said that, we think that the benefits outweigh the costs. Writing provides a permanent record of students' thinking. The teacher does not have to respond on the spot but can instead study the responses to plan supports.

There are a number of ways to check for understanding through writing. Mr. Uribe, from the opening of this chapter, uses exit slips. You can also invite students to respond to a writing prompt at the outset of a lesson; this is a way to activate their thinking about the topic at hand and to determine if information and ideas from previous lessons have stuck. Further, students can be invited to respond in writing throughout the lesson. One way to encourage this is through generative sentences, which give students a word and a specific place in a sentence to include the word. Often teachers also add conditions, such as the length of the sentence (Fisher & Frey, 2007).

Figure 4.3 contains some guidelines for creating generative sentences. For example, in the biology class for which students created the word map for *cell*, the teacher asked students to write a sentence with the word *cell* in the third position and include at least eight words total in the sentence. Here are some examples the class generated:

- *A plant cell is stationary, unlike an animal cell.*
- *A plant cell is composed of cellulose and hemicellulose, pectin.*
- *Most animal cells are very small, invisible to the naked eye.*
- *The plant cell is not like the animal cell because of its parts.*

Analyzing these sentences allows the teacher to assess students' vocabulary knowledge as well as their command of grammar. This analysis should lead to additional instruction that students need to master the content and language of the lesson.

Incorporate digital writing prompts

There are all kinds of ways of using writing in a digital environment to check for understanding. A shared platform like Google Docs (www.google.com/docs) can facilitate examination. Unlike conventional, one-way writing, students can use this platform to invite others (peers and teachers) to read, respond to, and edit their work.

Digital writing prompts to check for understanding might include the following (of course, many of these can be used with paper and pen or pencil as well):

- *Admit slips.* At the start of class (or a text or a unit of study), students write on an assigned topic such as "What was the most important point from yesterday's discussion?" or "Explain the difference between sedimentary,

FIGURE 4.3
Prompts for Generative Sentence Activities

Prompt Type	Examples
Letter placing	• Word that begins with _____. • Word that contains _____. • Word that contains _____ in the _____ position.
Generative sentences	• Begin a sentence with _____. • End a sentence with _____. • Create a sentence with _____ in the _____ position.
Word limiting	• Provide a range (e.g., 8 to 10 words in length). • Provide a minimum (e.g., at least 5 words in length). • Provide a maximum (e.g., no more than 11 words in length). • Provide a specific length (e.g., exactly 8 words in length).
Sentence patterning *(Parts of speech)*	• Begin a sentence with a noun. • Use a proper noun in a sentence. • Use a noun and a pronoun in a sentence. • Include an adjective with a target word. • Use an adverb in the third position in the sentence. • Include a preposition in your sentence. • Use _____ as a gerund. • Use a noun infinitive to make an interesting sentence.
Sentence patterning *(Punctuation)*	• Write a sentence that ends with an exclamation mark. • Ask a question using the word _____. • Write a sentence with an independent clause and a semicolon. • Use a colon with a list. • Include a parenthetical expression in a sentence.
Sentence patterning *(Elements of style)*	• Write an imperative using the word _____ . • Create a sentence with a prepositional phrase. • Use a possessive with the target word _____ . • Begin a sentence with a dependent clause. • Write a sentence that uses alliteration. • Use _____ as a simile. • Include an appositive in a sentence with the word _____ .

Source: From *Scaffolded Writing Instruction: Teaching with a Gradual-Release Framework* (p. 94) by D. Fisher and N. Frey, 2007, New York: Scholastic. Adapted with permission.

metamorphic, and igneous rocks." Reviewing student responses lets you know if there are students who already understand the content, or if there are confusions you still need to address.

- *Found poems.* Students reread a text and find key phrases that are important to meaning, and then they arrange these phrases into a poem without adding any of their own words. This type of prompt allows you to check students' understanding of key ideas from a text.

- *Take a stand.* Students share their opinions about a controversial topic based on their reading. For example, students might respond to the prompt "Zoos are humane places for animals" after having read articles on both sides of the issue. These prompts provide teachers with information about students' ability to articulate opinions, evaluate and make written arguments, and supply evidence.

- *Letters.* Students write letters to others, including elected officials, family members, friends, people who have made a difference, and so on. For example, you might have students respond to the prompt "Write a letter to Abraham Lincoln informing him of the current issues regarding racism in our country." This type of prompt also allows you to check in with students regarding their engagement with and understanding of the topic.

- *Exit slips.* Used at the end of a lesson, students write on an assigned prompt such as "What I want to inform my parents about this experience," "Three big ideas from the text," or "Three plausible actions the character may take in the next chapter." Exit slips are useful when you want to know what material stuck and if there are misconceptions following a class session.

An important advantage of writing to and with students in a digital environment is that the feedback you provide is less likely to be lost. We have always been puzzled about the timing of written feedback to students. Many teachers expend tremendous effort writing feedback on summative assignments, and relatively little on formative ones. But these small, low-stakes written assignments are where your feedback is most essential, because it's actionable. When you provide comments or direction while the unit of study is under way, students have opportunities to strengthen the writing and the content knowledge the writing is expressing. Digital student folders give them a place to store your written feedback and examine it again as the unit progresses.

Use personal blogs

Another way to use student writing to check for understanding is through the use of personal blogs. Davis and McGrail (2009) described their efforts in teaching 5th graders to blog, noting that students produced their best writing when the world was their audience. However, issues about student privacy and security are quite real, and providing a safe, restricted environment where the content can be monitored is essential. Many learning management systems such as Edmodo and Haiku provide a way for teachers to establish classroom blogs that are password-protected and allow only approved participants. A commercial blogging service called Kidblog (www.kidblog.org) provides a controlled environment so that the teacher can establish and monitor a classroom blogging community.

Fourth grade teacher Jeremy Liang uses blogs to foster digital citizenship and global connections about the books he and his students are reading. He has partnered with 4th grade classes at Department of Defense schools around the world to create a blogging community to discuss what they are reading. His class and a 4th grade class in Germany read *Soldier's Secret: The Story of Deborah Sampson*, a narrative about a woman who disguised herself as a man in order to fight in the American Revolutionary

War. Many of the children in both classrooms had mothers serving in the military, and Sampson's story intrigued them. Using the blog, they discussed the book and shared additional information culled from the National Women's History Museum and the Canton (Massachusetts) Historical Society. "I was really amazed at what they ended up doing with this," said Mr. Liang. "What started as a book club discussion grew into a collective investigation, with both classes vying to uncover another nugget about her," he said. "I thought I knew a lot about her, but I was really blown away when the class in Germany found out that her husband was able to collect Revolutionary War spousal pay after she died, because [the U.S. government] said that the war didn't have a better example of female courage than her," he said, shaking his head. "These kids have moms and dads who are courageous, too, and that really resonated with them."

Use tools designed to support emerging writers

A good tool to use to check for understanding via writing with very young children is Alpha Writer Deluxe (www.montessorium .com/alphawriter/). The program offers engaging illustrations and a simple pull-down letter system. Children write simple stories about their world and select the illustrations they want to use. The program is designed following the learning theories used in Montessori education, meaning that the tools are self-paced and designed to encourage exploration. Children learn to build words that parallel the same developmental practices of emergent writers, namely writing phonetically. This feature makes Alpha Writer a particularly good choice for checking writing progress; the program does not correct spellings, giving the teacher insight into how students are expressing themselves. Transitional kindergarten teacher Laurie Washington uses Alpha Writer to check on her students' writing development. "I like using this one because it doesn't alter or correct what they write. It lets me see what they're doing in real time." Ms. Washington used a field trip to a local farm as inspiration for their writing. "They worked together to choose illustrations, then sounded out the words for the story. I met with partners to discuss what they learned from the field trip, then asked them to tell me about the digital writing they did," she said.

Use Projects and Portfolios to Check for Understanding

Individual daily lessons often include short assignments that provide information about students' current learning; these can be used as a source for formative assessment data. But longer projects and performances can also be an excellent window into students' present state of learning. They can be a challenge due to the amount of time that they can consume, but when paired with student self-assessment, projects and performances provide particularly valuable insight into students' cognitive and metacognitive processes.

Tanya Emeka took this approach while teaching her 3rd graders to conduct research on their own. "This is a new set of skills for them," she explained. "They've had experience with participating in shared research projects in the lower grades, but now they're trying these skills out for themselves." Ms. Emeka paired a round of short research projects with existing science content. "We've been studying the solar system, and now students are locating information about the planets, moons, and asteroids, and of course, the sun," she said. "This is a good research project for them to conduct because the topics are well defined."

An earlier research project on the countries of the world—the students' first—taught Ms. Emeka a lot about the state of their skills and where they needed to go next. For that assignment, she met individually with each student to identify a country that he or she wanted to learn about and then used Sweet Search 4 Me (http://4me.sweetsearch.com) to set up a search engine that would only return sanctioned sites. "I learned from this experience that very few of the kids had well-developed Internet search skills," she noted. "Mostly, they searched by typing in the name of a country, so they didn't get the kind of info they were looking for." Armed with the formative assessment data she gleaned from the last project, Ms. Emeka spent time teaching search skills in preparation for the solar system research project. "This time around, I have them identifying keyword search terms to match the questions they wrote about the topic," she explained. "I've also taught them some simple techniques, like putting meaningful phrases in quotation marks. I'm already seeing a difference in the quality of the information they are finding. As I am conferring with them, I'm including questions about how they are finding sources."

Student production of information is as important as their consumption of it, and projects provide an excellent means to be able to gauge how students are applying and extending content knowledge. However, the days of shoeboxes and trifold cardboard displays are numbered, as more and more teachers are finding digital spaces for students to demonstrate what they know. Glogster, a digital poster system (http://edu.glogster.com/) allows students to use video, audio, text, graphics, and images to create online experiences crafted by them on any topic. A 6th grade social studies teacher we know uses Glogster's classroom feature to allow students to view one another's projects. "I'd never have enough wall space for the 180 students I see every day, but I can set these up by period. I require the kids to view and comment on five other projects completed by their classmates, and I review every student's project *and* every student's comments on *other* projects as part of my grading," she explained.

The Seesaw digital portfolio (http://web.seesaw.me) is designed to provide online display and viewing space for younger students. The app allows children to take photographs of their work and add accompanying voice or text explanations. They can curate their work to demonstrate their learning, and a teacher can view items as they are added. First grade teacher Zara El-Amin receives a notification each time one of her students adds an item to his or her portfolio. "I learn so much about them each time I see what they have determined is representative of their learning," she remarked. "Sometimes I'm puzzled by what a child chose, which tells me I need to talk with her to find out why she picked a piece to include." Ms. El-Amin said that aside from gathering formative assessment data, the digital portfolio is useful when she is conferencing with parents, because it provides insight into learning over a longer period of time. "Sometimes a parent is worried that their child isn't making good progress, but the portfolio allows me to show them how the child's skills are evolving. Sometimes, it's the opposite, where I can show the parent areas of concern," she said.

Second grade teacher Sarita Hernandez uses Flipagram (http://flipagram.com/) in the weekly parent newsletter she constructs with her class. A rotating group of students takes photographs all week to document events and the learning content, then edits and assembles the digital photos into a 30-second slideshow accompanied by music. The links to these Flipagrams appear in the parent newsletter, along with short explanations written by those assigned to the journalism team for the week. Ms. Hernandez's 2nd graders have used Flipagram to document field trips, the hatching of the classroom's chick, and their efforts to create a map of the surrounding community. "The families like these because they get to see what's happening in the classroom, but I like it even more because it gives my writers and storytellers an authentic reason for doing this work," said Ms. Hernandez. "We have a production schedule, and it has helped students organize their work time because they know they have deadlines. And I get to see the work in progress, so there's lots of opportunities to do just the kind of 'fix-up teaching' that a child needs."

Performance samples, like portfolios, refer to some form of student work that serves as an artifact for reflection by teachers, students, and parents. The original use of the term *portfolio* came from the collections of best works maintained by artists and architects. In education, portfolios typically consist of samples that represent particular types of tasks over a period of time rather than the student's best work. Examining samples of work that come from everyday settings rather than from test settings helps teachers determine when—and where—their students need further instruction.

As with all assessment, portfolios require clearly defined goals and purposes, data collection that traverses time and task, and a system of interpretation. When there is confusion about portfolio purpose, teachers wind up with collection bins of random student work. One way to establish clear purpose is to develop the expectations for the portfolio with students, working together to brainstorm selection criteria for portfolio inclusion and list the types of pieces that serve as evidence of mastery.

Typically, students with a history of poor achievement are not excited about gathering and reflecting on their work. They've likely had a number of opportunities to see how poor their performance is. When teachers provide clear success criteria and monitor progress, being sure to recognize students' perseverance and persistence, these types of assessment can change students' understanding about their performance and their ability to complete tasks. Portfolios can provide hard-to-teach students with evidence of their progress that they can directly observe.

Although the purposes of the portfolio shape its particular organizational structure, some standard elements are advisable for any portfolio to be used in formative assessment, including

- A table of contents
- Samples of daily work
- Drafts and revisions of written work
- Student self-evaluations
- Goals written by the student, teacher, and family
- Student-teacher conference records
- Other observational data collected by the teacher

Portfolios are a powerful example of the recursive nature of assessment and instruction. When used well, they not only aid in the teaching of new skills but also support the continued polishing of students' metacognition through guided reflection.

Foster Goal Setting

The act of conferring with a student in a one-on-one setting can have a considerable positive effect on both participants. In particular, students who have struggled with school have not typically had the opportunity to meet with a teacher who got to know them; most of their interactions with well-meaning adults are focused on remediation, telling them answers, or encouraging them to try harder. And then there is the simple reality that supportive conferences in which students are encouraged to set goals and reflect on their progress are all too rare in busy classrooms. Conferences may be informal and relatively short (just a few minutes), or longer, with a structured script of questions. Either way, the goal of conferencing with a student is to promote the student's own ability to assess and reflect. An example of a conferencing form appears in Figure 4.4.

Time is a teacher's most precious commodity, and finding opportunities to confer with students can be a challenge. Even so, setting time aside to talk with students one on one is a worthy investment. While the task of meeting individually with 35 or more students may seem daunting, teachers can set daily goals of conferring with only one or two students and make their way through the entire class over the course of a few weeks. Meetings might be conducted when students are working collaboratively in small groups or independently. Wise practitioners also recognize these meetings as a powerful tool for promoting student self-assessment and identity development, two factors that can be game changers for students with a history of struggle. Far too many students tell themselves that they are not good at school

FIGURE 4.4
Conferencing Form

Name of student: _____ Date: _____

Description of student work used in this conference: _____

_____

_____

Questions About Performance:

• What do you like about this piece?

• What would you change?

Questions About Process:

• What was the best strategy you used to complete this piece?

• What did you do when you had a problem with this piece?

Questions About Perception:

• What goals do you have for yourself this year?

• Have you achieved the goals you have set for yourself?

• What help do you need to reach your goals?

and look for confirming evidence of that belief. Changing the story that students tell themselves about themselves can begin the process of learning, motivating them to engage with learning at a whole new level.

In many classrooms, the primary evaluator is the teacher. On the infrequent occasions when students participate in the assessment process, their involvement is nominal, such as checking a fellow student's work against the answers the teacher has written on the board. It's rare to encounter classrooms where students are asked to identify goals and monitor their progress toward those goals, even though there is plenty of research attesting to the achievement- and motivation-boosting value of student goal setting and self-assessment (Hattie, 2009). This is not just a lost opportunity; it's a potentially damaging oversight, as exclusive reliance on externally driven assessment systems can have a negative effect on student achievement and attitude toward learning (Winograd & Paris, 1989).

Thankfully, educators have begun to take note, and in recent years, we've seen greater student involvement in planning and monitoring learning. The emphasis on brain-based learning is an example of such a development. Psychologists and neurobiologists have shown that the search for meaning is innate and that meaning emanates from the learner, not the teacher (e.g., LeDoux, 1996). Self-assessment opportunities in daily practice increase each learner's ability to seek and identify goals that are personally meaningful. Assessing one's progress and gauging next steps, with guidance from the teacher, are important for learning, especially as students grapple with setting time lines for completion, accurately estimating their work capacity, and resolving persisting difficulties. Figure 4.5 shows a self-assessment guide appropriate for upper elementary grades and above designed to be followed over the course of a longer project. Students plan and reflect at the beginning, middle, and end of the project, and self-assessment then becomes part of the project itself. In our

---

FIGURE 4.5
Self-Assessment Form for Project Performance

Name: _____

Before Project   Date: _____
My goal(s) for this project:

Steps I need to take to meet my goal(s):

Mid-Project Check-in   Date: _____
Am I on target for meeting my goal(s)?

What is my evidence?

What do I need to do in order to meet my goal(s)?

Project Completion   Date: _____
Did I achieve my goal(s)?

Why or why not?

What are the strategies that worked for me?

What will I do differently next time?

If I had one more day to complete this project, I would . . .

experience, students who are taught to plan and monitor their work habits begin to take ownership in their work and develop habits for completing complex tasks.

Use Assessment Data to Design Interventions

As we have noted, there are many ways teachers can routinely collect assessment data, but the challenge goes beyond collecting data to properly analyzing and acting on it. Many of us feel like we're swimming (if not drowning) in data. Those hard-to-teach students who struggle with learning and language are especially vulnerable to systems that value collection over analysis and action.

Likewise, there are many instructional approaches teachers can employ to help struggling students access content and make progress toward learning goals. But even with systems like differentiated instruction, small-group learning, and establishing purpose in place, and even with checks for understanding and one-on-one student work conscientiously incorporated into practice, some students will still demonstrate difficulty mastering skills and concepts. The truth is, holding high expectations for all students means inevitably that some students are not going to reach them. But getting frustrated with these students, or giving up on them, isn't going to provide the breakthrough results they need. It's not even on the table.

The solution is to use the data gathered through effective assessment practices to design instructional practices targeted explicitly for the students who need them. Response to instruction and intervention (RTI²), conceptually the same as Multi-Tiered Systems of Support (MTSS), is the careful examination of student learning and the educational program to test hypotheses, monitor progress, and identify instructional and curricular resources that put students back on track. The levels of RTI² include core instruction, but in practice this is often overlooked in the rush to begin intervention. However, core instruction is a key element in RTI^2 because the failure to examine the classroom context in favor of discrete intervention does a disservice to teachers and students, in that there is no plan for generalization and transfer. The most common organizational system includes three parts:

- *Tier 1 quality core instruction*, which includes assessing, instructing, and identifying learning difficulties in order to respond (e.g., modeling, reteaching, pre-teaching, differentiating instruction).
- *Tier 2 supplemental needs-based intervention* to provide further instruction on skills and concepts needed as background knowledge. Students receiving Tier 2 supplemental intervention are learning content their peers have already mastered but they have not. Students' progress is monitored to identify instructional techniques and curricular experiences that show promise.
- *Tier 3 intensive intervention,* which is used when Tier 2 intervention has not yet yielded a clear picture of which instructional techniques and curricular experiences will be the answer the student needs. Intensive interventions are often delivered through individualized instruction, with frequent assessment to monitor progress.

There are some misconceptions about RTI^2, so before we proceed, we will address them directly. One common misconception is that the purpose of RTI^2 is to "fix" a child, "catching him or her up" with same-age peers. In truth, RTI^2 is an inquiry cycle designed to figure out how to best meet the needs of the specific student. The purpose is right in the name: we are looking for a child's *responsiveness* to the instruction and intervention. We don't want to try a mishmash of approaches and then discard them too soon or stick with them too long, when in fact they might have been successful at the right level of duration, intensity, or frequency. In medicine, potential pharmaceuticals are repeatedly tested to identify the correct dosage. It isn't sufficient to say that a course of treatment is "good"; rather, the goal is to match it to the right patient conditions. The intent of RTI[2] is to properly match approaches that are well suited to the student.

A second misconception is that RTI[2] has no end. Schools that subscribe to this belief quickly learn that the demand outstrips their capacity. An RTI[2] cycle of inquiry is meant to be finite, often about 18 weeks in length, which roughly translates to half the school year. It's important to note that an RTI[2] cycle can be shorter, too. If effective approaches are identified sooner, all the better. The final outcome should be that high-impact instruction and curriculum are enacted within the classroom.

Frank Humphrey has several students in his 4th grade class who have benefitted from his school's approach to RTI[2], and the supports he provides to his students are more precise because of it. Basra, whose first language is Somali, has benefitted from direct instruction designed to fill in gaps in her background knowledge. As a student with interrupted schooling experiences prior to her arrival in the United States two years ago, Basra is still piecing together content knowledge in mathematics. "She was in an RTI[2] study when she was in 2nd grade because she wasn't making the progress her teacher expected in math," said Mr. Humphrey. "Ms. D'Angelo worked with the English learner specialist to figure out what was going on. Pretty soon they figured out that when Basra took a short quiz at the beginning of a unit, Ms. D'Angelo could determine if she was missing any critical background information. I'm still doing the same thing, although as time has gone on and Basra has more experience with consistent, formal education, those knowledge gaps are getting more infrequent."

Second grade teacher Janelle D'Angelo has students in her class who are also getting intervention based on past RTI² inquiries. "The children in the primary grades are monitored for their reading progress, of course," she said. "In the final quarter of 1st, 2nd, and 3rd grades, we implement intensive interventions to the four or five lowest readers in the class, based on the March benchmark assessment." An examination of the specific children who receive these supports varies somewhat from year to year. Some students receive the intervention each spring for all three years; others only need to participate once or twice. "We call it the reading booster shot," she said. The teachers in these grades meet daily with identified children for eight weeks, providing supplemental instruction coupled with frequent reading and writing assessments. "We're accomplishing two things," Ms. D'Angelo explained. "We're ramping up skills through daily instruction, and monitoring their progress closely so we can pass on our findings to next year's teacher." Her school's results are notable.

In comparing progress overall, the students who initially participated in the intervention averaged 65 percent lower than their peers on a 1st grade criterion-based measure of reading. By the third year of this intermittent intervention, these same students were only 17 percent lower on a measure of reading, suggesting that the achievement gap had narrowed considerably (Frey, Lapp, & Fisher, 2009). Although this intervention technique hasn't completely closed the gap, "it's keeping them in the game," Ms. D'Angelo said. At a time when the gap typically widens in the first years of school (Chall & Jacobs, 2003), struggling readers at her school are reversing the trend.

Schools who successfully implement an RTI² inquiry cycle to accelerate student learning do so because they have adopted a systems approach. In other words, they don't leave the work to individual teachers and specialists who are toiling away in isolation. By putting these practices into place schoolwide rather than using a piecemeal approach that misses many students, these schools are able to seamlessly meld instruction with intervention. The result is an enhanced RTI² system that reflects the school's core mission—to ensure that all students achieve (Fisher & Frey, 2010). Here is a closer look at those schoolwide practices.

Collect screening data on all students

There are any number of tools that can provide screening information about students so that teachers can quickly identify students who might need supplemental instruction or intervention. Well-known tools include DIBELS and AIMS Math, but existing data may be overlooked. At the middle and high school where two of us work, each grade level team looks at the results of the state standards test from the previous spring to identify students for further support.

Involve families in analyzing data and planning for instruction

Once students have been identified through the screening process, meet with individual families to review results and brainstorm ways to provide supports. Depending on the context, there may be plans for small-group instruction in class or more formal intervention work before or after school. Families are instrumental in the success of an RTI² inquiry cycle, and involving them early in the process signals the school's desire to partner with them.

Recruit other adults

Most schools have experienced conventional RTI as a failed initiative because the needs soon outstrip resources. This is undoubtedly true when responsibility falls on the shoulders of just a few people (often the special education staff, instructional coaches, and specialists). But RTI² is something every teacher should participate in. Targeted supplemental interventions that use needs-based grouping can occur in every classroom. Typically, such intervention can be accomplished with targeted students while the rest of the class engages in collaborative learning. In addition, every certificated member of the staff who does not have classroom responsibilities can work with a few students who need Tier 3 intensive intervention. For example, a counselor may work with students who need behavioral interventions, while the school media specialist may provide intervention in content areas. It is vital that moving to this model involves everyone, especially administrators. The principal with a math credential can provide Tier 3 intervention to a student who needs work on developing number sense in algebra. This is leading by example, not decree.

Monitor progress data

Because so many adults are involved, it is necessary to provide an accessible data management system that everyone can access. Some student data management systems allow for this, but an easier route may be to set up cloud-based spreadsheets that make it possible for teachers and administrators to input and analyze data. Remember that you're looking for positive trends, not mastery, to figure out what needs to be integrated into the classroom.

Celebrate success

Make sure that families know about students' progress, and share information with other teachers who are not directly involved. Keeping people apprised of the progress and including them in the celebration of successes are ways to change the tone of the intervention. RTI² shouldn't be viewed through a deficit lens (e.g., "What's wrong with this kid?"). Rather, it should be seen for what it is: a tool for continuous school improvement that asks, "How can focusing on this student help our school improve?"

• • •

Assessment should drive instruction. Teaching is really a recursive process in which data are analyzed and lessons are developed, implemented, and monitored. In this chapter, we have focused on checking for understanding in a variety of ways using a number of different tools. From there, the teaching and learning process starts again. Importantly, as we have noted throughout this book, students who are hard to teach are likely to need additional instruction to master expectations.

Language Instruction

Rafael Aquino, the principal at Roosevelt School, had seen English learners become more proficient in spoken English as they moved through the grades. In fact, some students became quite capable of understanding and expressing themselves in English at a basic level in a matter of weeks or months and achieved intermediate fluency in a year or two. But Mr. Aquino also knew that everyday social language differs from the academic language found in textbooks, complex texts, class assignments, and tests. Students learning English must master both in order to access and communicate content-related ideas, successfully complete academic tasks, and raise their achievement levels.

Mr. Aquino was also concerned about the native English speakers on his campus who continued to underperform when compared to peers. Suspecting that a lack of academic language skills was a common barrier for both English learners and the underachieving native speakers, he arranged for teachers in his school to participate in a book study of the SIOP Model (see Echevarría et al., 2017) to better understand how to bolster students' ability to use the academic language.

In our experience, poorly developed language skills are at the core of many of the academic challenges experienced by English learners and struggling students. Because academic language development is the foundation of literacy and academic success, it is the responsibility of every teacher—ESL specialists and classroom teachers alike. Although a math or science teacher may not think of herself as a "language teacher" and an elementary teacher may think of language teaching as belonging solely within "language arts time," each content area has general and discipline-specific language that can and must be taught if we want our struggling students to develop grade-level proficiency in language, literacy, and content skills.

The teachers at Roosevelt learned that academic language is different in structure and vocabulary from everyday spoken English. It is more abstract and grammatically dense, it contains complex sentence structures, and, in addition to challenging subject-matter vocabulary, there are terms such as *analyze, interpret, use resources*, and *find evidence*. Many students who speak English well have trouble comprehending the academic language required to be successful in school.

Before learning about the differences between social and academic language, some teachers at Roosevelt mistakenly believed that students who spoke English well but did not perform well academically weren't putting forth enough effort, weren't motivated, or didn't care about their grades. In other words, they blamed their students for not completing work rather than recognizing that, more often than not, it was because their students couldn't understand or use academic language well enough to meet teachers' expectations. In fact, one math teacher commented that he had 34 students, 12 of whom were English learners. Eleven of these 12 were failing, and the one who was passing was getting a *D*. When it was suggested that there were things he could do to help these students, the teacher was skeptical. A couple of months after participating in the SIOP book study, he had seen the light: "You know, you taught me a lot. We weren't ready for these kids, and we were doing these kids a disservice" (Echevarría, Short, & Vogt, 2008, p. 153).

Another issue in play at Roosevelt School was that many teachers subscribed to the myth that there is a window of opportunity for learning language and one's language-learning ability diminishes with age. Young learners actually do have an advantage in pronunciation and may be less self-conscious about speaking a new language than older children and adolescents, but older learners have their own advantage: a range of language experiences to draw on and integrate into their English language learning, especially in the areas of vocabulary and language structure. As teachers at Roosevelt began to understand the research, they realized that older learners are also better able to use memory strategies, word associations, and other devices to make sense of new language and add it to their linguistic repertoire. They became more open to focusing on language growth in their students once they understood that individuals are capable of becoming proficient in a new language at any age (Baily & Pransky, 2014).

Struggling students need teachers who take action to provide systematic academic language instruction in content classes as well as during a separate time designated for language development. In this chapter, we explore what this commitment looks like. Without question, all students who are not making expected progress can benefit from language instruction, and many of the practices discussed in this chapter can also be successfully used with native English speakers. But because language instruction is so critical for English learners, who face the formidable challenge of mastering a new language as they attempt to concurrently master new academic content—what Short and Fitzsimmons (2007) call doing "double the work"—it makes sense to stress the research and practices that have a positive impact on this growing population of students. Like the other chapters, this one is framed as recommended action items:

- Design language instruction to accelerate student growth.
- Integrate language teaching into content instruction.
- Leverage peer collaboration for language development.
- Target academic language growth.
- Create specialized and explicit language instruction for English learners.

Design Language Instruction to Accelerate Student Growth

The term *academic language* tends to elicit ideas about teaching vocabulary to students so that their reading, writing, speaking, and listening proficiency improves. Although having a robust vocabulary is necessary for academic success, academic language comprises more than vocabulary. Academic language encompasses oral language development, correct grammar usage, genre knowledge, classroom discourse, and other skills related to literacy, including foundational reading skills (Short & Echevarría, 2016). Academic language is fundamental to the study of disciplines such as math, science, social studies, and English/language arts, and it varies by discipline, as seen in Figure 5.1.

There are general academic terms used across content areas such as *demonstrate, define, analyze, element, compare,* and *category,* and content-specific terms such as *addend* and *exponent* for math; *bacteria* and *photosynthesis* for science; *demagogue* and *hemisphere* for social studies; and *metaphor* and *simile* for English/language arts. Each discipline also varies in the way information is presented and the text structures that are used. As students move from subject to subject, they encounter different types of discourse, and these differences should be explicitly

FIGURE 5.1
Discipline-Specific Academic Language

Discipline	Sample Discipline-Specific Vocabulary	Discipline's Common Text Structures or Styles
Science	Alchemy, allele, decompose, gamete, igneous, lenticular, nebula, organelle, radian, vertebrate	Information is presented in a logical order, and meaning is built up step by step.
History/Social Studies	Anachronism, artifact, bourgeoisie, chorography, diplomatics, humanism, paleography, stratigraphy, transhistoricity, typology	Text is literal narrative, and information is presented in chronological order but may also have embedded cause–effect and problem–solution explanations.
Math	Absolute value, algorithm, bisect, collinear, deciles, diameter, geometry, hexagon, parallelogram, solution set	Mathematical explanations have a logical and rhetorical structure, and the language is nontemporal (there is no past, present, or future) and very precise.
English/ Language Arts: Fiction	Allegory, connotation, diction, fable, irony, nemesis, oxymoron, personification, stanza, verse	Fiction, or narrative text, is usually straightforward. It contains a beginning (introduction of the characters, setting, and the main problem), a middle (contains a rise in action as the main character tries to solve the problem), and an end (the problem is solved).

taught. When students understand *how* things are said in each discipline, they can better understand *what* is being said.

Language is needed to communicate ideas, information, and concepts; the ultimate goal of explicit academic language teaching is academic success for English learners and struggling students. With a mindset of urgency, teachers employ techniques that will accelerate and advance students' language proficiency. There are a number of ways to accelerate growth, and we'll look at some critical ones now.

Develop language profiles

Just as you wouldn't waste precious time teaching phonics to a fluent reader, you want to teach struggling students and English learners what they need to learn and not what they already know. To save time and avoid frustration—for you, for students, and for teachers down the line—early in the school year, assess each student's strengths and areas for improvement in order to determine aspects of language development that warrant more or less attention and create a language profile that will follow that student from grade to grade.

Many states use formal measures for designated English learners, and these instruments yield valuable language profiles. However, many other students who struggle with academic language development do not have language profiles. We've developed a short interview format for you to use with individual students to gain a sense of how they use language in school and at home (see Figure 5.2). We encourage you to use this as an interview protocol rather than a survey, as conversing with students individually provides a rich opportunity to gauge their skills, strengths, and areas for growth.

For English learners, instruction that capitalizes on their first language is most effective. Research shows that literacy and other skills and knowledge transfer from one language to another (Goldenberg, 2013); in other words, once something is learned in one language, it can be accessed in another language or more easily learned in the new language. In lesson planning, 3rd grade teacher Ken Parsons consistently thinks of ways to tap into what his English learners know and can do in their home language and link it to lessons taught in English. One favorite activity is to create bilingual books on a topic the class has studied. His students

FIGURE 5.2
Questions for a Student Language Profile

Language Use at School	Always or Mostly True	Sometimes True	Almost Never True
I like to learn new words and use them when I talk and write.			
When I learn a new word, I try to use it as much as I can.			
I make up new words when I don't know the right word for something.			
People at school tell me when I say something incorrectly (e.g., they correct grammar or pronunciation).			
I get nervous when I have to speak in front of a group at school because I am not confident about my language use.			
I understand my school subjects, but it is hard to express my ideas about the topics I am learning about.			
Language Use at Home	Always or Mostly True	Sometimes True	Almost Never True
I am able to express my ideas at home clearly.			
I tell my family about my day at school.			
I am able to understand and follow directions at home.			
I tell jokes and stories at home.			
I write notes at home to my family.			

read the completed books to students in younger grades. Students with less proficiency use more pictures in their books, but all students are able to talk about their book in English and their home language.

Consider foundational skills gaps

Academic challenges for some English learners and struggling students can be rooted in weak foundational literacy skills. Whatever the grade level, students who have not yet mastered one or more aspects of literacy—phonics and word recognition, for example—need to be provided instruction and practice in these skills.

Although Arleta Garcia teaches 7th grade English, she spends time with a small group of students who struggle with comprehension. While the rest of the class is working on their own assignments, Ms. Garcia explicitly teaches the group comprehension strategies to strengthen their skills. Making time to teach explicit, focused lessons on foundational skills is sometimes difficult to do, but Ms. Garcia realizes that many students get passed along from grade to grade without the kind of explicit teaching they need to become strong readers and writers. Because her preparation as a secondary teacher didn't include how to teach foundational skills, from time to time, she collaborates with elementary grade teachers for additional teaching. She's fortunate in that her school does provide high-quality materials for English learners and struggling students that include an explicit focus on foundational skills in all grade levels.

Keep critical thinking skills at the center

Just because English learners and struggling students may have difficulty expressing themselves doesn't mean they cannot think critically. High school U.S. history teacher Omar Daniels uses skillful questioning to elicit higher-order thinking, but he accepts responses that are consistent with each student's proficiency level. For example, he asked a beginning English learner, "In comparing urban growth in New York and Los Angeles, which of the factors listed [pointing to the list] had the greatest impact? Why?" The question requires critical thinking, but by showing a list of factors that were discussed, he reduced the linguistic load for the student. The beginning English learner gave a simple reply but did so while pointing to an illustration or information in the text to demonstrate his understanding of the concept. Now let's contrast Mr. Daniels's question with one that's more typical of those asked of English learners and struggling students: "Which city had the fastest growth rate during the last century, Los Angeles or New York?" Simple recall questions like this one are easy to come up with but don't require the student to do any critical thinking. Anyone asked this question has a 50/50 chance of guessing the right answer. There's no call for higher-order thought processes such as evaluating, comparing, and synthesizing information.

Build on what students bring

All students arrive at school with a repository of experiences, knowledge, preferences, and abilities. Too often teachers have a deficit view of students who are not achieving at or above grade level, meaning they focus on what these students aren't doing rather than look for what they can do. Formal assessment results notwithstanding, each student has skills to build on and interests to tap into. In order to build on what students bring, teachers must get to know their students. What is Jackie interested in? What is Javier good at? What does Showen like best about school? The easiest way to find out about students is to ask. Provide sets of prompts such as these: *The best part of reading is____. The worst part of reading is _____. One thing I want you to know about me is _____.* Use the information garnered from these questions to inform your planning and teaching.

Integrate Language Teaching into Content Instruction

In 2000, when the SIOP Model first popularized the practice of including language objectives in content classes, some content teachers were resistant to the idea. However, educators are now more aware of their responsibility to teach language along with subject matter. This is due in part to the increase in the number of English learners in schools at a time when rigorous state standards have increased academic language demands for all students. In our own work, we have seen that English learners and hard-to-teach students can participate fully in content lessons when attention is given to the way the lesson is taught and to the language needed for learning the content (Echevarría, Richards-Tutor, Canges, & Francis, 2011; Short et al., 2011). In content classes, although the focus is on learning subject matter and related skills, language development takes place simultaneously through well-planned lessons.

Although designing instruction to include built-in academic language supports benefits every student in a classroom, it benefits struggling students with limited language proficiency most of all. What we're talking about here are differentiated written, verbal, teacher-provided, or peer-provided supports that facilitate expressive language use (i.e., help students express themselves while speaking and writing) and strengthen receptive language skills (i.e., provide support for listening and reading). We recommend using these supports as a way to simultaneously make content instruction more understandable for all students while teaching discipline-related language and language usage (Vogt & Echevarría, 2008; Vogt, Echevarría, & Washam, 2015).

Use language frames to guide content-focused thinking and conversation

Language frames scaffold participation and provide learners with ways to organize their thinking and express themselves more clearly. Frames have become a common practice and are particularly effective as supports for writing and speaking tasks. The sentence frames should be adjusted for various levels of language proficiency so that students are using language that is just beyond what they could do independently. In Frank Casey's middle school math classes, he supports math conversations by providing frames like the following, which help students notice and describe their mathematical thinking and solution strategies:

For beginning English speakers:

The strategy I used was _____.
(Choose from this list: counting-on, double facts, doubles plus one)

For more fluent speakers and other students:

I agree with [student's name], because the strategy allows us to _____. Your strategy reminds me of [strategy or procedure].

The frame for beginning English speakers provides words from which students choose, reducing the linguistic load. The more advanced frames allow students to extend their expression and use the ideas of others by linking them to solutions and strategies.

Mr. Casey prints these frames on table tents, and during conversations, any student who wants to consult them can do so easily, although students are encouraged to use frames appropriate for their language ability. Some students develop their own frames or have integrated this type of thinking and speaking into their habits.

Mr. Casey has also posted other language frames that focus on specific types of academic thinking and language use. For example, extended word problems are vexing for all his students, who struggle to determine what information is needed and what is not. Mr. Casey created a poster called "Finding Relevant

Information" that provides a number of helpful language frames like these:

I believe this information is relevant because _____.

I do not need _____ to solve this problem, because I'm being asked to _____.

The problem is asking me to solve _____. This is necessary in order to complete the computation of _____.

Use cognates to help English learners access prior knowledge

Mr. Casey also uses cognates—words that share a common root—to support learning for English learners who speak Spanish as a first language. For example, *diferencia* and *difference*; *para comparar* and *to compare*; and *capacity* and *la capacidad*. Mr. Casey isn't a fluent Spanish speaker, but he consults and uses discipline-specific cognate lists available online. Providing these kinds of supports gives his English learners a way to access background knowledge that might be relevant to the lesson and helps them understand the lesson's foundational ideas (Coggins, Kravin, Coates, & Carroll, 2007).

Cognates should be used judiciously in multilingual classrooms because they may not be equally useful to all students, depending on the number of home languages you have in your English learner population. In the right context, however, they can be a good choice. Mr. Casey knows that many of the English learners in his class attended schools in Mexico and Central America and received instruction in mathematics. He is capitalizing on their knowledge of academic Spanish to leverage content learning in English.

Create content-specific word walls to build academic vocabulary

Word walls are bulletin boards, charts, or other visible areas that contain a collection of high-frequency or theme-related words that are used to teach vocabulary. The posted words are used as a reference during activities, since students need multiple exposures to words before they "own" them. Word walls have been found to build and strengthen high-frequency word vocabulary (Jasmine & Schiesl, 2009).

In Mr. Casey's classroom, he keeps a running record of mathematical language organized by unit of study. As he introduces terms that require definitions and explanations, he jots them on a surface that can be preserved (e.g., a PowerPoint slide or a length of butcher paper) for reference throughout the unit of study. He adds simple drawings to illustrate each word and create context. For instance, during a unit on probability and statistics, his word wall included terms such as *independent variable, dependent variable, ratio,* and *stem-and-leaf plot.* He also encourages students to contribute words to the word wall so that it becomes a richer, more relevant resource as their knowledge expands. When the unit is completed, the terms are transferred to another section of the room to serve as a visual library of previous areas of study.

Leverage Peer Collaboration for Language Development

Learning is a social endeavor. Although people can and do learn "on their own," learning through interactions with others, both in school and out of school, is an essential skill and a vital part of life experience. Sometimes, this collaboration is as simple as sharing ideas and hearing those of others. At other times, it means creating something new in partnership with others.

Peer collaboration—or group work—has gained currency as a 21st century skill. It certainly has great value in language instruction, because it requires students to use and listen to others using academic language. But setting up collaborative activities requires more than simply pushing a few desks together and hoping for the best. Group work requires deliberate planning to ensure that it is aligned with task goals and supports the learning processes students need to use to arrive at answers (see Chapter 2).

We think of group work in two broad categories: *basic group work* and *productive group work*. Both are necessary and of value, but each is less effective when it's not well matched to the learning task. Both types have two elements in common—student interaction and opportunities to use academic vocabulary and language—but they vary in other important ways.

The purpose of basic group work is to share information, ideas, and beliefs. These are language functions and are essential for crafting language objectives for a lesson. Students engaging in basic group work are not solving anything or producing anything; they're just sharing ideas, responses, and reactions. There is either no accountability or group accountability only. Teachers use basic group work routines all the time, especially when we ask students to talk with one another for a few minutes.

In contrast, productive group work is focused on resolving problems, coming to consensus, or identifying solutions. These are language functions as well, but notice how the language demand is more complex than those required for basic group work. Productive group work requires longer periods of interaction because students are working to create something substantial. Another hallmark of productive group work is that everyone is individually accountable for his or her contributions. Individual accountability raises the stakes for students, because they can't sit back and let others do the work without consequence.

As noted, both types of peer collaboration have a role to play in language development.

Employ basic group work routines

Sometimes, teachers want students to clarify their thinking and to practice the academic language of the lesson. In these cases, basic group work routines work perfectly well. These routines provide time for student-to-student interaction and peer support. As we have noted throughout this book, students need to produce language, not just consume it. These brief opportunities to interact with another person builds students' academic language in a fairly stress-free environment (e.g., Frey et al., 2013). Here are some common basic group work routines you can use to simultaneously support language learning and content learning.

The **Turn to Your Partner and—** prompt invites students to talk with a peer about something that the class is discussing. For example, as part of a discussion about World War I, students might get this prompt: "Now that we've finished reading our texts, turn to your partner and discuss what you think was the main cause of the Great War."

Think-Pair-Square, a twist on the familiar Think-Pair-Share, invites students to think about a topic, discuss it with a partner, and then share the dyad's thinking with another partnership. For example, as part of a discussion in earth science, students might be asked to talk with a partner about the effects of tectonic plate movement and then share that with another group.

There are a number of variations for the **Novel Ideas Only** routine. In general, the goal is for students to come up with original ideas that no one else has expressed. For example, as part of their review of a chapter that was read aloud, the students in Maxwell Swanson's 10th grade English class were asked to write down three key details from the text. Mr. Swanson then asked all of the students to stand and began calling on individuals at random to share a detail. As the students listened, they checked off any item shared by another person; when all three of their items had been checked off, they sat down, regardless of whether or not they had spoken. Sitting students took on the responsibility of judging whether each detail shared was novel or a repeat. The activity continued until there was just one person left standing.

Opinion Stations are based in conversation and reflection. Sometimes it's useful for students to talk with others who have the same opinion because it allows students an opportunity to deepen their understanding and acquire new ways to express their ideas and opinions. Typically, the teacher labels the corners of the classroom: *strongly agree, agree, disagree,* and *strongly disagree.* Students are invited to move to the corner that represents their thinking about a topic the teacher presents and talk with others there. For example, the students in Olivia Cruz's art history class learn about aesthetics and how they individually define beauty. Ms. Cruz often shows her students a piece of art, typically projected from a museum website, and invites them to move to the corner that represents their appreciation for the piece. She poses the premise that the piece belongs in a museum or collection, and they can agree or disagree with this statement, discussing why they believe so using the academic language of artistic appreciation. She asks that their conversations include key vocabulary as well as specific reasons for their appreciation—or lack of appreciation—for a specific piece of art. As an added step, Ms. Cruz asks students to "fold the line," which means meet with someone who has a different opinion from theirs. "The Opinion Stations provide students an opportunity to clarify their thinking while using the academic vocabulary of our discipline," Ms. Cruz explained.

Employ productive group work routines

In order to increase academic language proficiency, students need the opportunity to engage in active listening and speaking (Short & Echevarría, 2016). The research base is clear that oral language development is a key factor in reading performance (Wolf, 2008), and spending the majority of the instructional day passively listening while others talk will not give English learners and other struggling students the language development they need. Like basic group work, productive group work routines allow students to interact with their peers using academic language. However, unlike basic group work, productive group routines hold individuals accountable and require that each student participate in the collaborative effort. In addition, productive group work provides the teacher with evidence of each student's learning that can be used to guide future instruction.

At the beginning of every school year, Aalya Pavri teaches her 5th grade students how to participate in productive discussions while using academic language. To that end, she explicitly teaches the meaning of targeted vocabulary words at the outset of a lesson so that students will use those words and reinforce their understanding. Each group has a discussion rubric that provides an incentive for students to use the vocabulary words in context. During peer discussions, Ms. Pavri circulates among the groups asking about the rubric and checking to see if students are using the vocabulary terms.

Students can also be taught routines for productive discussion that they can learn to follow with little teacher supervision. Bondie, Gaughram, and Zusho (2015) suggest two effective discussion routines that stimulate purposeful conversations: Elbow Partner Exchange and Homework Rounds. Both also offer great opportunities for language development.

An **Elbow Partner Exchange** involves two students who engage in discussion about a topic related to the lesson. For example, given a math problem, they might list on a sheet of paper the questions they have about the problem or note possible solution strategies. When they've finished, they sign their names. Then the student pair exchanges this information with another set of partners, who address the previous pair's notes— answer the questions listed, for example, or add their ideas to the existing thoughts on solution strategies. They also identify their contributions by signing their names. The teacher who reviews the Elbow Partner Exchange sheets can zero in on what students already know and what they need to learn. In doing so, students practice academic vocabulary and are apprenticed into crafting increasingly sophisticated sentence structures. They also clarify their own thinking as they have an opportunity to hear the perspectives of their peers.

Ms. Pavri uses **Homework Rounds** as a way for students to correct homework assignments together and discuss when their answers differ from one another's. Students document their suggestions and ideas on each other's papers and identify themselves by name. Through the discussion, they may come to an understanding of the mistakes that were made so they can avoid making the same ones again. These homework assignments are then submitted to the teacher, who gains a record of the extent to which peers are able to support each other's learning. The teacher can also flag which individuals will benefit from reteaching. Again, students are producing language and getting practice in academic conversations. In the case of Homework Rounds, they're also able to ask for assistance with difficult content and explore answers and the reasons they got those answers.

Let's look at a few other common productive group work routines that promote integrated content and language learning:

In a **Conversational Roundtable**, each student folds a piece of paper into four quadrants and then folds the center down as a triangle (see Figure 5.3). As they read a piece of text or investigate a problem, they take notes in the first quadrant, under their name. When the group members have completed their notes, they meet to discuss their thinking. As each group member shares his or her notes, the other members write the speaker's name in an empty quadrant and record key points. When the

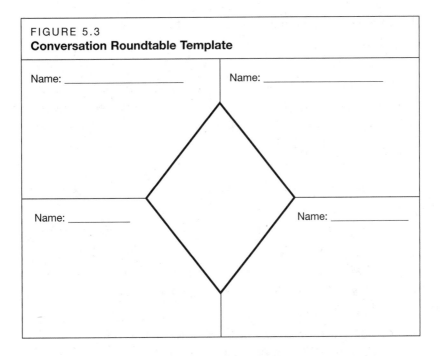

FIGURE 5.3
Conversation Roundtable Template

group discussions are finished, each student writes an individual summary of the conversation in the rhombus in the center of the paper. Fourth grade teacher Matt Ingersol uses a collaborative roundtable to provide student accountability in group discussions to ensure each is contributing and getting academic language practice opportunities. He can quickly assess students' individual understanding by reading their summaries and trace where conversations went wrong by reading each students' initial thinking and notes from others.

In a **Collaborative Poster** session, students work in groups to create a poster representing a concept, text, or topic they are exploring—often following a provided rubric that describes elements that must be included. After thinking individually about how to represent their ideas, each student selects one color of pen and uses only that color on the poster paper. All students must contribute to their group's poster in writing and by drawing, and then sign it. When students in Jeffrey Evans's geometry class created collaborative posters, everyone was required to propose one step in a proof and then provide an explanation. Mr. Evans was able to walk around the room, checking for understanding. The color of the ink on the posters showed him which students were contributing which ideas, giving him insight into academic language use as well as conceptual understanding. In this way, he could see which terms students were using and, with the help of a few follow-up questions, was able to get a good idea of students' level of understanding.

In a **Jigsaw,** each student in the class is assigned to a home group and an expert group. The activity begins with the home group meeting to discuss the task and divide it into subsections, according to the teacher's directions. (Jigsaw is especially useful for reading text that is sectioned, with each section able to stand alone.) After the members of the home groups have completed their specific task, all students move to their expert groups, composed of members who completed the same task component. The expert groups read and discuss their portion of the assignment and practice explaining or teaching it to other members. Finally, students return to their home groups, teach their portion of the work to other members of their group, and learn about the other sections of the work. Jigsaw provides students with access to the ideas and perspectives of their peers as they talk about the text. In doing so, students spend time with language, taking turns talking about the content of the lesson.

Fourth grade teacher Andrea Miller often uses the Jigsaw technique with her students as they read sections of the textbook collaboratively. When students meet with their expert group, the discussion focuses on understanding the content; when students meet with their home groups, the focus of the conversation shifts to sharing that understanding. Because these discussions require a focus on a specific type of academic language use, Ms. Miller provides language frames for students to apply. For example, finding and citing text evidence requires particular terminology. Therefore, she has a set of language frames for using evidence-based terms and lists phrases like these:

According to the text . . .
The author says . . .
For instance . . .
Based on the reading, I concluded . . .

Figure 5.4 shows additional routines that facilitate language development through collaborative peer learning.

FIGURE 5.4
More Productive Group Work Routines to Facilitate Language Development

Routine	Procedure
Barrier Games	One partner has a picture or information that the other partner does not have. Students sit back to back or have a visual obstruction to block their view (a barrier). Using oral language only, students communicate to complete the task. Tasks may require partners to draw a picture, place objects in specific positions, find the differences between two pictures, and so on. Students in small groups might each have one picture in a sequence. Without looking at the other pictures, they must collaborate with their teammates to put all the pictures in the correct order.
Busy Bees	Students mimic the buzzing sound and slow movement of bumblebees as they buzz around the room to find a partner. When the teacher says, "Busy bees, fly!" students move around room and buzz until they hear, "Busy bees, land!" The "bees" standing closest together become partners for a brief learning activity, such as giving an opinion or answering a question.
Collaborative Dialogue	In groups, students write a dialogue that highlights and extends their understanding of the topic. Characters in the dialogue may be human or not (e.g., positive and negative numbers discussing why they can't get along). Students must use the assigned vocabulary. All students participate in an oral presentation of the dialogue, regardless of the number of characters or students in the group. They may read chorally or take turns playing a role or find another way for all to participate.

(continued)

FIGURE 5.4 *(continued)*
More Productive Group Work Routines to Facilitate Language Development

Routine	Procedure
Explorers and Settlers	Assign half the students to be explorers and half to be settlers. Explorers seek out a settler to discuss a question about the topic. Each partner shares his or her thinking and can take notes as appropriate. Repeat the process a few times so that students can either get different perspectives on the same questions or discuss a new but related question each time.
Find Someone Who . . . or Walking Review	Students must find a classmate who can answer a question on a handout. They ask this classmate the question, and then write down the response they are given, along with the classmate's name. This can be done as a review of learning or in anticipation of learning. It can also be done Bingo-style.
Fishbowl	A group of students models a strategy or task. They sit in the middle of the room (in a "fishbowl") with remaining students seated around them. Students in the fishbowl engage in the task, with the teacher providing guidance as needed. It's wise to give observing students outside the fishbowl a purpose for listening, such as completing a graphic organizer, writing down a quote or two, or listening for specific examples.
Inside/Outside Circles	Two concentric circles of students stand or sit and face one another. The teacher poses a question to the class, and the partners respond briefly. At the signal, the outer circle rotates one position to the left so that each student is facing a new partner. The conversation continues for several rotations. For each rotation, students may respond to the same prompt or to a different but related one.
Numbered Heads Together	Each group is assigned a number, and every student within that group is assigned (or selects) a number from one through four (or five, if the class size necessitates it). The teacher asks a question, announces the start of a short discussion period, and reminds the class that every student in every group should be prepared to provide the answer. At the end of this discussion period, the teacher spins an overhead spinner and announces the number of the student who will be called on to respond. Groups have one more minute to make sure that number student in their group knows the answer. The teacher spins again and announces the number of the group that must respond.

FIGURE 5.4 *(continued)*

More Productive Group Work Routines to Facilitate Language Development

Routine	Procedure
Reciprocal Teaching	Students work in groups with a common piece of expository text. Each group member has a role— summarizer, questioner, clarifier, or predictor—and these roles mirror the kinds of reading comprehension strategies necessary for understanding expository text. The reading is chunked into shorter passages so that the group can stop to discuss periodically, with each student performing his or her role in the discussion.
Study Buddy Teaming	Students work first in pairs and then in teams of four to share and compare answers, practicing the processes of collaboration and coming to consensus. Students work with their Study Buddy to read text, solve a problem, or answer a question. Once the Study Buddy pair has completed the work, they team up with another pair to form a Study Buddy Team. The teammates shares their work, compare and justify answers, and come to consensus on the final product. Products may be presented to the whole class.
Think-Write-Pair-Share	The teacher gives students a minute to think about a prompt and then a few more minutes to write down their ideas (typically in bulleted list or note form, without focus on spelling or grammar). Next, students share their ideas in pairs, listening carefully to what each partner has to say. A few pairs will be called to share with the whole class, and students must be prepared to share and explain their partner's ideas.
Three-Step Interview	Students work first with a partner and then in a team of four to respond to a question. Questions may relate to opinions or be at any level of Bloom's taxonomy. It is helpful to have each pair respond to a different question so that the sharing does not become repetitive and boring. Follow this structure: Step 1: Partner A interviews Partner B while Partner C interviews Partner D. Step 2: Partner B interviews Partner A while Partner D interviews Partner C. Step 3: Partners A and B tell Partners C and D what their partner said, and Partners C and D tell Partners A and B what their partners said.

Sources: Fisher, Frey, & Rothenberg (2008); Vogt, Echevarría, & Washam (2015).

Target Academic Language Growth

Academic language growth doesn't just happen; wise teachers know that they must create the opportunities for their students to use the language of the classroom in their speaking, listening, reading, and writing and provide supports so that students do so successfully.

The approach we recommend is to integrate collaborative conversations into each lesson, provide (and fade) instructional scaffolds to build competency, provide visual aids to augment abstract academic terms, and assess formatively and frequently. We'll explore each of those components in turn.

Teach collaborative conversations with intention

Language supports such as sentence frames and word walls are helpful, but to really advance struggling students' academic language proficiency, teachers need to get these students involved in academic conversations. Not only do these conversations promote instructive interaction, in which students can learn from how their peers are using academic vocabulary, but they also provide students critical practice opportunities to use those terms themselves, pulling in not just the language that is the focus of the current lesson but language from previous lessons as well.

It's true that effective collaborative conversations require careful planning and structure, but we have seen remarkable discussions and student contributions take place under the right conditions. Research (e.g., Fisher et al., 2008; Short & Echevarría, 2016; Zwiers & Crawford, 2011) supports the following practices:

1. Plan for purposeful talk in every lesson.
2. Note and convey to students the language demands of the lesson's discussion as well as its content objectives.
3. Explicitly teach the rules for discussion and reteach these rules regularly.

4. Prompt discussion by designing effective questions and conversation tasks to spur strong thinking.

5. Teach students how to pose questions and respond to the questions of others.

6. Develop a learning community that does not depend solely on the teacher to mediate discussion.

7. Hold students accountable for their participation in small- and large-group discussions as well as for their mastery of the content.

Use (and fade) instructional scaffolds

Effective instructional scaffolds are appropriate scaffolds— sufficient to provide students the support they need to engage in the classroom and with the content. Keeping scaffolds appropriate, then, means scaling them back as students become more skilled and require less intensive support.

In the previous example of Mr. Daniels's lesson about urban growth, he used a number of scaffolds that he varied to suit the proficiency levels of his students. You'll recall that Mr. Daniels asked a beginning English learner, "In comparing urban growth in New York and Los Angeles, which of the factors listed [pointing to the list] had the greatest impact? Why?" Importantly, he allowed sufficient wait time for the beginning speaker to formulate his thoughts and answer. Mr. Daniels provided other scaffolds for some of his other students to support their participation, including language frames and graphic organizers. However, Mr. Daniels is interested in having his students make progress. "I've learned not to fall into the trap of routinely providing the same language scaffolds in May that I was offering in October," he said. "I meet with students periodically throughout the year to discuss what scaffolds I've been providing and talk with them about our plans to fade them."

As his students develop their expressive and receptive language skills, the scaffolds Mr. Daniels provides are less intensive.

For instance, he expects more proficient students to generate responses that go beyond the sentence structure of the language frame provided. He prompts higher levels of expression through questioning to elicit more complex language as he sees their capabilities rise. And he provides less wait time between questions and responses. Over time, he explained, the interaction between himself and his developing English speakers comes to resemble the patterns of conversations of native English speakers and others who are proficient with the language of the classroom.

Provide visual supports

One of the very real challenges of acquiring academic language is that so many of the concepts students encounter are abstract ones. It's downright challenging to grasp the movement of tectonic plates or why multiplying fractions yields a smaller number simply by reading a text description. Fortunately, visual supports can be a great help in clarifying abstractions for students who may struggle to understand for any number of reasons, including interrupted schooling, poor preparation in prior grades, limited English proficiency, or poor reading comprehension.

We recommend making use of the plethora of resources available to augment text. Easily accessible digital multimedia sources provide myriad resources for photographs, illustrations, and videos teachers can show to support students' academic language learning. We definitely believe carefully chosen YouTube and TED Talks have a role to play in the modern classroom. High-quality curricular programs also provide a wealth of visual resources as publishers recognize the changing demographics in schools and respond accordingly.

Assess performance frequently

The practice of routinely checking for understanding and analyzing the results to make decisions about what is taught next—formative assessment—has been discussed in earlier chapters, but we would be remiss if we failed to note the vital role of formative assessment as it applies to academic language learning (Fisher & Frey, 2011).

Third grade teacher April Hightower uses formative assessment to gauge student comprehension and adjusts her teaching based on the results. She does this routinely through quick-writes, short quizzes, student group responses, interactive journaling, and conferencing. She has learned from experience that unless she knows where her students are in the learning process, how they access information most efficiently, and where the gaps in their learning are, she can't advance their language and literacy development the way she wants to or in the way they need in order to meet high academic standards.

Create Specialized Explicit Language Instruction for English Learners

Students who are learning English as a subsequent language need specialized language learning opportunities in addition to those outlined throughout this chapter (Short & Echevarría, 2016). Research indicates that although incorporating language instruction into content lessons benefits this population, they also need a time each day when language instruction, provided at their level of English proficiency, is the sole focus (Saunders & Goldenberg, 2010). This kind of explicit language instruction is typically referred to as English language development (ELD) or English as a second language (ESL), and it is considered subject matter in its own right. That is to say, it should not be confused with English/language arts or sheltered instruction. ESL or ELD instruction may be delivered in a number of ways, such as by a specialist who pushes into the classroom or by the classroom teacher while the rest of the class is engaged in other work. What is most important is that it is focused language teaching that occurs every day.

There are a variety of standards that can be used to guide instruction during designated ELD/ESL. Teachers utilize these standards for lesson planning and teaching. Although ELD/ESL is the primary focus during these sessions, it's taught within the context of content so that important knowledge and concepts are reinforced through language practice.

Best practice for designated ELD/ESL is to provide continuity by working with the vocabulary and concepts from English/language arts lessons. English learners require multiple exposures to words and ideas in order to make literacy and language gains, and the repetition during designated language study provides the necessary intentional redundancy (August & Shanahan, 2010). When English learners return to whole-group teaching after having had ELD instruction, they are more likely to be able to participate in core lessons with their English-speaking peers.

Because learning a new language is a social process developed primarily through meaningful and motivating interactions with others, the emphasis of designated ELD is on use of language with peers rather than knowledge *about* language, per se (Saunders, Goldenberg, & Marcelletti, 2013). With this in mind, we'll turn to specific ideas for developing English language and literacy. Although the four language domains—reading, writing, speaking, and listening—are best taught in a fully integrated way, we will discuss examples by focusing specifically on two areas—*reading and writing* in the first example and *speaking and listening* in the second—in order to provide more specific suggestions.

Offer specialized reading and writing instruction

As we mentioned earlier, it's likely that English learners at all grade levels will need instruction in foundational reading skills. Designated ELD/ESL is the ideal time to provide this. We suggest pairing reading instruction with a focus on writing as a way to help readers become better at both. After all, both reading and writing improve through practice and feedback.

In our experience, modeling reading and writing strategies and habits, paying attention to the skills students have yet to master, and providing explicit instruction and practice to target these areas is a reliable way to improve student performance.

Kendra Monroe takes this approach when supporting the language and literacy development of her 5th grade English learners. As they read a story or informational piece, she stimulates students' imaginations and supports their reading comprehension by providing a buffet of ideas and strategies from which they can choose.

During reading, Ms. Monroe chunks the text into manageable parts, then pauses to ask questions, prompt discussion, and check for understanding. She jots down words and ideas to highlight for students. Sometimes she takes these notes and models how to present them in a graphic organizer of ideas. Other times she turns them into sentence frames or brings up synonyms and antonyms for some of the words in the passage and then lists them in a T-chart.

Ms. Monroe has found through experience that this type of exercise is time well spent. In addition to providing time for academic language instruction and practice around a content topic, she is modeling for students how to take words and ideas and turn them into usable products. Essentially, she is laying out "prepared dishes" on a "buffet of ideas." When the time comes to complete tasks and writing assignments, rather than assembling everything from scratch, her English learners can work with the various strategies she's created and modeled for them. And she's also helped them make sense of the text.

Offer specialized speaking and listening instruction

Lina Niño teaches 4th grade in one of the lowest-performing schools in her district. Eighty percent of the school's students are economically disadvantaged, and nearly 40 percent are designated as limited English proficient (LEP). The following example took place during a literacy lesson, but it offers an excellent idea of the kind of teaching appropriate for designated ELD/ESL time. Although the lesson focuses on writing, it is anything but a strictly paper-and-pencil activity. Ms. Niño incorporates multiple opportunities for students to practice speaking and listening skills.

Before students write about a topic, they create a storyboard and then share it orally with a partner. As students tell their story to a partner, the partner asks questions about parts that are unclear or out of sequence. They talk together to fill in gaps and create a more coherent story. Then the partner shares his or her story and follows the same process. After the partner work, Ms. Niño tells students to write their stories just like they told them to their partners.

Ms. Niño models the writing process herself by telling a story of her own to the class as students listen, and then she writes it to provide students with a mentor text. Ms. Niño reads several students' stories as the class listens. While she reads students' original pieces, Ms. Niño flags common errors and later teaches minilessons to explicitly teach correct language usage. Her students have an opportunity to talk about the skill focused on in the minilesson and students offer suggestions for improving stories she reads. Then students rework their writing, incorporating the skill they learned. She provides practice opportunities until students have mastered the specific skill.

Since she adopted this approach, Ms. Niño's 4th grade students have made significant progress. Fifty-six percent of her students achieved a "commended" performance on the district writing test, meaning they earned a score of 3 or 4 on the test's 4-point scale. The district's overall LEP population had a commended rate of 19 percent, and its total student population had a commended rate of 34 percent (Echevarría et al., 2015). Ms. Niño's writing development approach is one that incorporates plenty of opportunities for speaking and listening.

• • •

Learning is based in language, and the root of many of our hard-to-teach students' struggles is language deficiency. As such, we believe that every lesson at every level, kindergarten through high school calculus, should include both explicit and embedded language instruction. We are not suggesting that all teachers teach reading, but we do believe that all teachers need to consider the linguistic demands of the content they teach, make it transparent to students by designing and posting content and language objectives, and focus on language consistently and systematically. We have seen the difference this makes (Short et al., 2011). You'll see it, too.

A Supportive Climate and Culture

Entering Charles Lindbergh School, the sign over the main entrance is impossible to ignore: *Love is spoken here.* The principal, Mr. Gaioni, is out front every morning, greeting students and family members. "Good morning, how are you?" he says. "Buenos días! Good morning!" These greetings are repeated many times. The students who enter the building are smiling and seemingly happy to be at school.

Inside Charles Lindbergh School, there is a large, colorful sign posted next to each classroom door welcoming you to the specific teacher's class. The hallways are vibrantly decorated with student work along with various posters and bulletin boards that convey positive messages. *Welcome to Lindbergh School: A Great Place to Learn!* one says. *Kind words . . . for you, for me, for Lindbergh!* says another. *No Place for Bullying* announces a third.

Inside the main office, where families come for information and to conduct school business, there is a Spanish-speaking community worker with a bright smile. "How can I help you?" Mr. Carlos asks every person who enters the office. Above his desk is a student-made sign that says, *Mr. Carlos is the best!!* It's an indication of how staff, parents, and students feel about him.

Charles Lindbergh School is not a well-resourced building. It was built in the early 1900s and is located in a high-crime, high-poverty urban area. Although the facilities are old, the school climate is refreshingly upbeat and positive. Of Lindbergh's nearly 900 students, 57 percent are English learners. There is a palpably positive atmosphere and demonstrated mutual respect among teachers, students, and families.

The culture and climate of effective schools like Lindbergh don't "just happen." They are carefully constructed and maintained through continual attention. We use these two terms—*culture* and *climate*—deliberately in order to capture two different but related concepts. Both are essential considerations for anyone trying to reach students who are hard to teach.

A school's *culture* describes the collective behaviors, procedures, and practices that reflect the organization's beliefs and values. These include the written and unwritten rules that govern daily operations. In the case of Lindbergh, the culture is supportive and positive, as exemplified by the actions of administrators and staff. Their belief that every student and family member is an important part of the learning community is apparent in the way that teachers welcome families and address them by name and in the principal's practice of greeting students at the gate each morning. In the simplest terms, school culture captures what people in the school *do* to express what matters to them.

A school's *climate* captures the way its culture feels to everyone who experiences it. Climate describes how staff, students, families, and community members perceive what goes on during the school day (Smith et al., 2015). Even the best intentioned initiatives and research-supported practices will not thrive if the climate is inhospitable. And, generally speaking, the climate becomes inhospitable when initiatives or practices aren't implemented or communicated as well as they should be.

The culture and climate that students experience in school is perhaps as critical to their learning as the instruction they receive. Are they safe, and do they *feel* safe? Are they valued and respected, and do they *feel* valued and respected? Are their family members welcome, and do they *feel* welcome? For students we think of as "hard to reach," the answers to these questions are usually, and unfortunately, no.

Culturally diverse students who are chronically disengaged report that they lack positive relationships with teachers and are aware of disrespect toward their culture or ethnicity. This is an important point to linger on—it is the relationship *with individual teachers* that defines their perceptions of the school as a whole. In other words, what we do in our classrooms has a direct and lasting impact on whether a child or adolescent believes he or she is held in high regard or not. In this way, each classroom either enhances or detracts from the school's overall culture and climate.

When we speak and write about culture and climate, we sometimes hear from frustrated teachers who tell us, "I like your ideas, but I'm only one person. I can change what I do, but I can't change the whole school." We believe that responses like this undervalue the impact one person can have—especially if that person is a classroom teacher. The culture and climate of every classroom creates the culture and climate of a school.

Decades of research have shown that the most significant influence on a child's achievement is the teacher (Allen et al., 2013; Elliott, 2015; Hattie, 2009). It's not poverty, it's not personality—it's the teacher. How great is that? We absolutely make a difference in the learning lives of our students. The culture we build and the climate we create is integral to their achievement. And schoolwide achievement is built classroom by classroom, by individual teachers like us. We just need to do it.

To establish the kind of supportive culture and climate that will make a positive difference for struggling learners (and all learners), here are the actions we recommend:

- Create positive student–teacher relationships.
- Build cultural competence.
- Assess your classroom culture and climate.
- See the value in diversity.
- Manage the dynamics of difference.
- Institutionalize cultural knowledge.

And the very good news is this: All of these actions are well within your grasp.

Create Positive Student–Teacher Relationships

Even the most skilled and content-knowledgeable teacher can be ineffective when the relationship with a student is rocky or distant. As we have noted before, learning is a social endeavor. The teacher's connection with the student is the catalyst.

While the importance of student–teacher relationships has been chronicled countless times in the education literature, it is generally considered more often in elementary instruction. This is unfortunate, because the evidence on its importance in middle and high school is equally strong. Marzano, Marzano, and Pickering (2003) performed a meta-analysis of studies on the influence of positive student–teacher relationships and found that the effect size in middle school was nearly double that in elementary (2.89 vs. 1.6). These findings are echoed in the work of Allen et al. (2013), focused on identifying effective interactions in secondary schools. Consider this report:

> The magnitude of the strongest prediction, from the Emotional Support domain, indicates that, after accounting for all other measured variables, a student entering with average prior test scores (i.e., 50th percentile) in a class that was one standard deviation below the mean in Emotional Support would on average place at the 41st percentile on end-of-year tests: whereas an average student with the same background characteristics in a class one standard deviation above the mean

would on average place in the 59th percentile in end-of-year tests. (p. 86)

Let's quickly unpack this quote. The researchers defined "Emotional Support" across three constructs: positive climate, teacher sensitivity (i.e., responsiveness to students' academic and emotional needs), and regard for adolescent perspectives (i.e., "the teacher's ability to recognize and capitalize on student needs for autonomy, active roles, and peer interaction" [p. 81]). In other words, then, a teacher's warmth, caring, and demonstrated regard for students plays a measurable and vital role in the academic performance of students. And this means *all students*, including those we may think of as hard to teach.

Effective teachers seek out opportunities to build positive relationships with hard-to-teach students, making sure that each day these students feel acknowledged and valued for who they are and what they bring to the classroom community. To be sure, there are students who vex us, and those who resist building relationships with an adult. But it behooves us to monitor our interactions carefully to make sure we aren't the ones sending signals that say, "Stay away." The chronically tardy student we greet with "I'm glad you're here; the place isn't the same without you" may understand over time that his absence is noticed and that he is missed. The girl who sits silently in the back of the class hoping to go unnoticed can benefit from us getting down to her eye level and speaking quietly and kindly to her. The boy who cracks jokes instead of getting to work can learn that a gentle hand on the shoulder, words of encouragement, and a bit of redirection can be channeled into an internal monologue that helps him self-regulate, stay on task, and enjoy learning.

Build Cultural Competence

The students who attend our schools represent the larger society in which we live. In the United States, and in many other countries as well, the population reflects an increasingly larger number of students who speak a different language at home; are first- or second-generation immigrants; live in poverty; or identify ethnically, racially, or socioeconomically as different from their teachers (Snyder & Dillow, 2015). Yet while the influences of home have a significant impact on student learning (Hattie, 2009), educators rarely leverage these "home factors" to meet the needs of students (Hernandez & Kose, 2012), despite evidence that attention to cultural competence has a positive impact on achievement, behavior, and student well-being (Jackson, 2009).

So if classroom culture is what we do, and classroom climate is how it feels, then it is reasonable to conclude that the school and classroom culture experienced by our increasingly diverse students must change to meet their needs. Although these practices and beliefs go by a number of terms, we will use the definitions supplied by Lindsey, Nuri Robins, and Terrell (2009):

- *Cultural proficiency* is a mindset, a worldview, a way a person or organization makes assumptions for effectively describing, responding to, and planning for issues that arise in diverse environments. For some people, cultural proficiency is a paradigm shift from viewing cultural differences as problematic to learning how to interact effectively with other cultures.
- *Cultural competence* is behavior that aligns with standards that move an organization or an individual toward culturally proficient actions. (pp. 4–5)

A major roadblock to teachers becoming more culturally competent is in remaining unaware of our own cultural influences. Although the U.S. student population continues to diversify, the demographics of the teaching force have not changed significantly in the past two decades: 76 percent of teachers are female, and 82 percent are white (Kena et al., 2014). These descriptors are not a measure of cultural competence, but they do indicate that the experiences of educators may not mirror those of their students and underscore the value of paying attention to cultural proficiency. Unfortunately, white teachers may be unaware of their own cultural experiences and how these influence their thinking; this leaves them ill-equipped to pick up on how school structures and practices may be perceived by others (Santoro & Allard, 2005). Arguably, it's this combination—teachers' ignorance of their own cultural influences and biases coupled with limited understanding of students' experiences—that leads to lowered expectations for some students, a deficit-thinking approach, and an incorrect assumption that certain kinds of homes are "chaotic" just because they are different from what the teachers know (Anagnostopoulous, 2003).

Begin with cultural sensitivity

We'll build out our lexicon just a bit further now with a third term—*cultural sensitivity*—which describes a logical entry point for building one's cultural competence. Cultural sensitivity is the awareness that the differences between the dominant school culture and individuals' own values and perceptions have a direct effect on learning and behavior. Cultural sensitivity is only a place to start, as awareness alone does not lead to positive change. However, without awareness, the change process will never begin. There are ways for school personnel to create an environment that values diversity and builds on students' different ways of learning, behaving, and using language so that students experience a culturally responsive school (Gay, 2010).

Charles Lindbergh School, which we described at the beginning of the chapter, is only one of many schools we know of where there is a commitment to creating a positive, nurturing, respectful climate inside and outside every classroom. Importantly, Lindbergh is not a monolith. It is composed of individual teachers who have invested in their own practice to become increasingly culturally competent. Lindbergh and other schools like it are committed to building culturally proficient educators who can leverage their understanding of the needs of culturally and linguistically diverse students, including English learners and students with disabilities. Are all schools like this? Unfortunately, no . . . but they *could* be.

Get introspective

After general awareness comes self-awareness. In *The Culturally Proficient School*, Lindsey, Roberts, and Campbell Jones (2013) suggest that the first step in achieving such schools is for individual teachers to examine their own behaviors and values.

Ask yourself these questions:

- Do you simply tolerate diversity in your school and class, or do you embrace it and learn from your students?
- Do you view changing demographics as a challenge, or do you see it as an opportunity to respond to the reality of the community?
- Are your teaching practices for English learners and other struggling students driven by compliance concerns, or are they driven by the desire for equity and to see all students learn and thrive?
- Are policies, procedures and practices for English learners and struggling students an "add-on" to existing ones, or are they integrated into a unified system that serves all students?

Lindsey and colleagues (2013) refer to the "A or B" distinction in these questions as *tolerance for diversity* versus transformation for equity. The next four actions we'll discuss borrow from and build on four essential elements of their Framework of Cultural Proficiency (Lindsey et al., 2009; Lindsey et al., 2013).

Assess Your Classroom Culture and Climate

The first element of creating a culturally proficient classroom is assessing its culture and climate. This means examining the procedures in place that influence the current culture and climate, reflecting on your own beliefs and biases, and listening to the voices of students' families to gain their perspectives.

Examine procedures in place and reflect on current beliefs and biases

Initially, 8th grade teacher Ryan Garcia, who grew up speaking English in a comfortable, middle-class home, interpreted the idea of assessing culture very narrowly. To him, it meant learning about what "those families" do and occasionally including activities that celebrate the cultures represented. He thought that by celebrating holidays and cultures, he was creating a classroom climate that was positive for his students. Other than on those occasions, though, his classroom procedures didn't take into account his students' different identities; he treated all students the same. But in time, and within his school's extended professional development experiences about cultural proficiency, Mr. Garcia discovered that assessing culture and climate meant that he first needed to take a look at his own attitudes toward diversity, many of which were based on stereotypes he developed early in his teaching career. "It was an uncomfortable moment of recognition when the presenter cautioned us to beware of people who use the term 'deal with' when describing children," he said. "I heard my own voice saying that countless times." This moment led Mr. Garcia to question other assumptions and biases he possessed and to engage in critical reflection and discussions with peers about his own cultural background and values. With his new insight, he also examined more carefully the way he set up and ran his classroom.

Mr. Garcia also began interacting more with families of his students and the community around the school, getting to know people as individuals rather than the stereotypes he once held. He knew from his own experiences that not all Latino families are the same and that not all Latin countries share the same culture. "But I never made that leap in understanding my students' experiences," Mr. Garcia confessed. "Some of my kids come from Islamic countries, but I just sort of lumped everyone together." Through personal outreach, he learned more about his students' home practices, values, and traditions, and some of what he learned led him to revise assumptions he'd made. For example, he used to get upset with "unmotivated" students who didn't have all their homework complete; then he learned that most students had family responsibilities after school which made it difficult to carve out a couple of hours for homework. He also learned that in many homes, there wasn't a quiet place to complete the extensive homework he assigned. These revised perceptions led to revised practices and procedures. "I used to rely heavily on discipline as a way of motivating my students to do the things that I believed were important for success," Mr. Garcia said. "But over time I've come to see that I was kind of butting heads with some of their cultural beliefs. Giving a lot of homework wasn't teaching them the self-discipline that I thought it would. Now I talk a lot more with my students and really listen to what their lives are like, to what's important to them. From there, I figure out how I can support them. It's made a difference for everyone. I'm not as uptight and frustrated as I used to be," he chuckled, "and my students are actually doing better now than they did when I used punishment as a way to try to motivate them."

Seek the perspective of families

When partnerships are built between the home, school and community, there are multiple benefits. As school staff develop authentic relationships with families and community members, they are better able to include policies that leverage students, their families, their languages, and other attributes as resources that will enhance the school's ability to help all students meet rigorous academic standards.

The goal of family engagement is not to inform families about classroom requirements and school policies but to gain partners for a mutual relationship. Ferlazzo (2011) suggests that engagement is best achieved by listening—listening to what parents think, dream, and worry about. He suggests making home visits, a practice that we have also seen have a profoundly positive impact on teachers, students, and families. By visiting a student's home, you learn things about the student that you wouldn't otherwise, including family context. In our experience, families appreciate this investment of time and effort in their child and are much more likely to go the extra mile to support a teacher who makes home visits.

The special educators at the middle and high school where two of us teach pay a scheduled home visit to every new student with a disability. These home visits are conducted in the summer before the student starts at our school, meaning that the first contact these families and their teens have with the school is on their own turf. Many of these new students are also culturally or linguistically diverse, which can magnify the hesitancies they and their families may have about starting at a new school. It's a measure of the gratitude these families felt toward our special educators that some remain in contact with the school for years after their child graduates.

Mr. Garcia, the 8th grade teacher introduced earlier, practiced listening to his students' families and learned a lot about their values and goals. He confessed that he was surprised by how strongly the parents felt about their children doing well in school; previously, he had shared the opinion that *these parents don't care about education*. After getting to know his students' families, he found just the opposite to be true, so he began communicating with them about ways that they could support learning at home. The result was improvements in his students' engagement and sense of belonging—their attitudes toward school became much more positive. This was borne out in the climate surveys he and his school administered several times a year. The time Mr. Garcia invested in getting to know his students and their families also paid dividends in classroom performance.

A study involving urban high school students enrolled in a credit-recovery program for failing students supports Mr. Garcia's experience. Its findings show that regular, personalized communications from teachers to parents have a significant impact on struggling students' chances for success in their classes, especially when the teachers' messages include specifics about what students can do to improve their work (Kraft & Rogers, 2015). This kind of information gives parents something to discuss with their children about how to improve in school. Improvement suggestions relayed to parents are particularly helpful when they include an action the student can take—such as an assignment or quiz to make up. The researchers emphasized that teacher–parent communication has great "underutilized potential" (p. 1).

Strong school–community partnerships that include families in school policies and practices also model for students and their families how to interact in a democracy and function effectively together (Lindsey et al., 2013). Mr. Garcia's school has more actively recruited representation of all constituencies in meetings, on committees, and in planning school activities; now, more perspectives were included. What's more, the school's (female) principal began to convene regular off-campus morning meetings for a group of parents—all mothers—who had never attended school functions before because doing so would mean being in the presence of men who were not relatives. "I don't know why I didn't think of this before," the principal remarked. "I just took it for granted that I wouldn't see these moms at school functions. But holding off-campus meetings allows me to hear from them firsthand, and the perspective has been invaluable."

In past years, the principal and staff had counted translating school communications into students' home languages as a measure of successful family engagement. After they committed to becoming a more culturally proficient school, however, they realized that all families wouldn't have a voice in their student's schooling unless all families had a forum for sharing their insights.

See the Value in Diversity

A second element on the path to becoming more culturally proficient comes from valuing diversity and changing one's mindset in order to see it in its proper light: as opportunity. Sometimes schools unwittingly develop an "us against them" mentality that manifests itself in subtle ways. Valuing diversity doesn't mean trying to understand *others* and improve communication with *them*; it means that when you encounter a culture different from your own, you recognize that culture as worthy of respect and take steps to adapt to it. In other words, valuing diversity requires teachers to try to identify and remove barriers between ourselves and our students. The following are some ways to demonstrate the value you place on diversity.

Show you care

There is a long-established body of research demonstrating that teacher attitudes and behaviors have a significant impact on student achievement and well-being. Students want to know that their teachers care about them and that they are not anonymous. As we've noted, the relationship between students and teachers is a pivot point that determines whether a student will thrive or fail, and teacher sensitivity to student needs is a statistically significant measure of effective classrooms (Allen et al., 2013). Kafele (2013) suggests that a teacher's attitudes and the learning environment that teacher creates is the key to helping all students achieve and have a positive attitude toward school.

Sixth grade teacher Judith McDonald would agree. She warmly greets all students by name as they enter class in the morning and asks brief personal questions that demonstrate her genuine interest in her students. She speaks to them respectfully, setting a tone of mutual regard and kindness that the students pick up on and exhibit themselves. The classroom is organized, with students sitting in groups of four to facilitate optimal interaction and collaboration within each team. Ms. McDonald doesn't need to call roll; she knows her students and which team each student is on, so a quick glance around the room tells her who is absent. Class begins with the Pledge of Allegiance followed by a brief review of multiple-meaning words in preparation for upcoming standardized testing. She encourages students with comments such as "I know you'll do well on the test because you're prepared. You've been working hard on these practice questions. Good effort!"

Honor student experiences

During the lesson, Ms. McDonald often poses a question about the lesson's topic. She asks her teams of learners to discuss the question for a specific period of time and then report their ideas or answers. English learners are encouraged to use their home language to clarify points or express their ideas to a more proficient English speaker who can scaffold their participation in the group discussion. Students are urged to examine the question from their own experience and tie it to the topic. For example, as the class discussed an article about the conflict in the Middle East, Ms. McDonald urged her students to think about their own neighborhood or family. "Think about a conflict you've experienced outside school, with a friend or someone in your family," she prompted. "What issues did each side have? I know sometimes it's hard to see the other person's side, so talk about that for five minutes, and then we'll think about how that relates to the article."

Ms. McDonald asked a group to share a conflict they discussed and made a T-chart with points for each side. The teacher is prepared to moderate the discussion, because sometimes students discuss difficult topics involving violence or gang retaliation. However, she recognizes how important it is for them to be able to openly discuss the realities of their own lives in class and use those experiences to better understand the topics they are studying. In culturally responsive classrooms, lessons incorporate students' values, beliefs, and experiences, as well as use of their home language, as Ms. McDonald does in her class.

Demonstrate mutual respect with your words

Our attitudes are often exposed through the language we use to communicate with students, and students typically respond in kind. Showing respect for students is important because it contributes to an atmosphere of safety, openness, and reflection. As Beaudoin (2011) notes, "This context is crucial for the brain to effectively process and encode academic material, as opposed to being preoccupied with emotional concerns" (p. 40).

In Ms. McDonald's class, the respect she shows her students through her speech is mirrored in the regard they show for her, including the effort they expend in wanting to do well on assignments and the respectful way they speak to her. She knows that sarcasm, for example, is a bad idea, so she doesn't use it and doesn't see it from her students. "Sarcasm isn't fair because it involves an unfair balance of power," she explained. "Think about it. A teacher can be sarcastic because she's wielding the power. But the moment a student is sarcastic, now all of a sudden it's disrespectful." Ms. McDonald's observations here are borne out in the research, and it's a critical point to stress. In their analysis of more than 1,500 office referrals in a large school district, Kaufman and colleagues (2010) found that middle school students in general, and African American middle school boys in particular, were far more likely to be sent to the office for being "disrespectful" than other subgroups. This is troubling given that being disrespectful, while disruptive, is not a violent offense, and a student who has been given an office referral once is much more likely to be referred to the office again in the future (Wright

& Dusek, 1998), is more likely to be referred for special education services, and has an increased likelihood of failing school (Tobin & Sugai, 1999).

As teachers, choosing our words wisely and being conscious of the impact our tone, facial expressions, gestures, and body language have on our students is profoundly important. In Figure 6.1 we contrast supportive language with insensitive

FIGURE 6.1
Insensitive Language vs. Supportive Language

Insensitive/Unacceptable Language	Supportive Language
"I see a bunch of you aren't doing very well."	"I think some of you may need help. Give me a hand signal if you want me to show you how to do this again."
"Please don't tell me you don't know how to do this!"	"It looks like we need to pause a minute and review what we did last week."
"No, you're spelling these words wrong. There's no *e* at the beginning of *school* and *statement*."	"I see you're borrowing from your home language by putting an *e* at the beginning of these words. In English, many words start with a consonant, like *school* and *statement*."
"You're going to have trouble on the test next week."	"Let me model a few more of these problems; then you can give it another try."
"Seriously? You didn't even show your work!"	"That's a good try, but I need to see how you got the answer. Please show me your work. "
"Haven't you been paying attention? You got this wrong again."	"Try again. Take a look at the first one you did. Thanks."
"Doesn't anyone know the answer? C'mon, guys!"	"Yani, thanks for volunteering."
"Well, at least one group has finished the problem. What about the rest of you?"	"I'll bet you're feeling very proud of yourselves for solving that problem together. Your hard work is paying off."

remarks that can have a tremendous negative impact on students' achievement and overall well-being.

Manage the Dynamics of Difference

Many teachers feel uncomfortable discussing sensitive issues related to race, religion, language, and gender. Jennifer Harden teaches high school in a school that has had an influx of Latino and black students over the past decade. Some of her fellow teachers and some of her students resent the changes in their school's population and make their opinions known. Ms. Harden gets upset when she hears negative comments made by her colleagues. For example, she wasn't sure how to reply when a colleague said about English learners, "Even a few of these students can be a headache." For years, Ms. Harden focused on keeping the peace in her classroom and promoting a positive relationship among her diverse group of students. When one of them made a rude or disparaging comment, for example, she was quick to respond with a mild correction like, "Robert, that's not kind. You need to treat others like you want to be treated." She often sought to point out the similarities between diverse groups of students in an effort to unite them and make everyone feel comfortable. However, her best efforts didn't seem to curtail the negative comments and tension in her class.

Create positive conflict

It is important for teachers to facilitate discussion about difficult topics and issues, even though the work can be uncomfortable (Cruz, 2015; Kidd, 2011; Lindsey et al., 2013). When Ms. Harden was lamenting the situation in her classroom with her friend, Audrey Hogan, who teaches elementary school, she learned about an alternative approach to urging students to "get along and be nice." Ms. Hogan explained that she challenges her students to talk about negative feelings and situations they're experiencing. And when she spots conflicts related to race, religion, gender, or other kinds of difference, she brings them into the light herself.

"Some of the kids were making fun of another child's accent," said Ms. Hogan. "I resisted the urge to chide or scold them. Instead, I started by depersonalizing the discussion a bit by saying something like, 'I'm thinking about what it would have been like for me if, as a young girl, my family had moved to another country, maybe in Asia, where English wasn't spoken in school. What would've happened to me?'" She has lots of multicultural literature in her classroom, so she chose a title that would fit the discussion, and then she read her students a story about a child in a similar situation, one who encountered rejection, ridicule, and economic hardship. Then Ms. Hogan put her students into groups that included a mix of ethnicities and provided each group with some guiding questions focused on how the character in the story might cope with the situation. "This was really effective," she explained. "Soon we were talking about strategies we all use when we're feeling ridiculed."

Ms. Harden thought about the ideas her friend had used in her elementary classroom and realized that these same principles could be applied in her high school U.S. history classroom. She made a concerted effort to identify current events that could serve as topics of discussion—ones that would resonate with her own students and help to diffuse misunderstandings through open communication. "Right now, we're looking closely at the unrest that has resulted from police shootings of young black men," she said. She encourages her students to be honest about their opinions, but she is careful to structure the discussions in a way that forces her and her students to confront their own experience—whether it's one of enjoying privilege and opportunity or of being disenfranchised from the mainstream. "We're drawing connections to other times in history where marginalized people stood up for their rights," she said, noting that this helps to contextualize historical events. "We talked about the economic boycotts led by Cesar Chavez in the 1960s to draw attention to an injustice and how these same tools are being used today. I'm amazed at how much more compassionate my students have become since confronting difficult topics and issues head-on like this," she said. Since she and her students began engaging in this kind of positive conflict, behavior issues in her classroom have declined to an all-time low.

Don't pretend to be colorblind

There is a teacher at Ms. Harden's school who takes pride in being a "colorblind" teacher. He says he's not bigoted because he treats all students the same and doesn't notice their differences in ethnicity, economic status, or language. What he doesn't realize is that ignoring the influence of culture and language is as harmful as overt resentment. The false notion of colorblindness minimizes differences at the expense of an individual's right to develop a sense of identity (Hernandez & Kose, 2012). Even more dangerously, this stance ignores student's differential levels of need (the topic of this book) and allows teachers to tell ourselves we don't need to provide access because we're treating everyone "fairly."

In contrast, Bao Chai deliberately draws her students' experiences, ways of knowing, standards of behavior, and family and community practices into her instruction. She talks openly about fairness. "We start the year together with an extended discussion of it," she said. "Usually they'll start by saying that fairness means everyone gets the same. Then I give them the CPR example." Ms. Chai tells her students about the time she was attending a public event, and a man standing nearby collapsed. She and another bystander used their CPR training to keep the man alive until paramedics could take over. "I tell my kids that if I had applied their definition of fairness, I would have had to give everyone CPR. It opens a door for us to take a close look at what others might need in contrast to what they might need and to talk about how fairness is about providing the kind of assistance that is needed," she said.

When a student's behavior is in conflict with Ms. Chai's expectations or those of other students, she has an open discussion about it rather than sweeping it aside and ignoring the situation. Rather than seeing differences as divisive or threatening, she seeks opportunities for mutual understanding, recognizing that those differences are part of students' cultural backgrounds and experiences and have an impact on how students learn. "I've had some training in restorative practices," she said, "and I use a circle for us to discuss what's happening and how we can resolve it." When her 3rd period math class struggled early in the year because of disruption and technology use, Ms. Chai asked a counselor trained in restorative practices to facilitate the conversation. "We ended up developing some expectations we could all live with," Ms. Chai said. "It's not like it's magic, but it's a shared agreement I can draw on when there's some drift away from the expectations." By the way, Ms. Chai's "colorblind" colleague continued to amass the highest number of office referrals on the staff. He is now meeting regularly with an administrator to address this issue.

Institute antibullying policies

Bullying is a complex issue that has been around for the ages but has been exacerbated by today's social networks. Bullying can include teasing, spreading rumors, excluding someone on purpose, and attacking someone physically or with words. When students are bullied, it can leave them feeling alone, powerless, and different from others. Sometimes, students are bullied because they *are* different, so their sense of belonging at school and in society is even more severely threatened.

There aren't easy answers to "solve" bullying, but creating a schoolwide climate of nurturing, warm relationships and mutual respect, as we've discussed in this chapter, has been reported as the action most likely to reduce bullying (Davis & Nixon, 2011). Some other ways to reduce bullying include getting input from staff and students on consequences for bullying; imposing clear, fair consequences, which makes cooperation and learning more likely; being consistent in enforcing antibullying rules; and looking for warning signs of bullying, such as friction between the same students or a student who complains frequently of stomachaches, avoids certain activities, or seems particularly withdrawn.

Today, the high school where the teachers we've highlighted in this section work is more culturally proficient than it once was. One indicator of its progress is the new, anonymous digital reporting system students can use to share concerns about bullying and cyberbullying. When teachers and staff manage the dynamics of differences in positive ways, it benefits not only the school climate but also life beyond school. As Kidd (2011) puts it, "Our classrooms can become models for creating a more socially just world as we bring families and their experiences into the classroom and discuss rather than avoid racial, cultural, and linguistic differences" (p. 229).

Institutionalize Cultural Knowledge

Individual teachers can and do make a tremendous difference when it comes to providing a positive culture and climate for students. However, to have a greater impact, practices need to become part of the school fiber. Administrators and teachers must work as a team to ensure that all students feel respected and accepted, and that they are held to high academic standards with supports in place to promote success.

Principal Phillip Izumi uses culturally proficient practices at Hoover School. As an instructional leader, he regularly observes classroom teaching to ensure that the rigorous, standards-driven curriculum is being implemented effectively, and that teachers are using research-validated approaches that provide English learners and struggling students with the supports they need to achieve academically (Echevarría et al., 2017). The curriculum at Hoover integrates multiple perspectives and uses textbooks that accurately and positively portray a variety of cultural, racial, and gender groups. Mr. Izumi encourages teachers to incorporate formative assessment, gathering information about each student's response to instruction and adjusting their instruction accordingly (see Chapter 4). Teachers at Hoover don't rely solely on nationally normed tests to provide information about students' academic performance.

Mr. Izumi also works hard to make sure that the school and classroom environment is dominated by positive regard for learning and making academic progress, not by standardized assessments. Although testing is important, Mr. Izumi recognizes that test results are most effective when viewed as feedback on teaching, not an indictment of students, and are used for the purpose of improving instruction to boost achievement.

Provide opportunities to expand students' experiences

As an "at-risk" student recently said, "We should be called 'opportunity students' because we are one opportunity away from doing well in school or dropping out; one opportunity away from having a job or being behind bars." Her perspective is quite profound, especially for such a young woman. But she also recognizes that she and so many of her friends would benefit in a life-changing way from the kinds of opportunities that other students enjoy. Many struggling students and English learners, especially those from low socioeconomic backgrounds, are not familiar with the multiple organizations that provide opportunities to participate in important causes such as social justice, charitable endeavors, or environmental and civil liberties advocacy. At Hoover School, Mr. Izumi institutionalizes opportunities to expand students' experiences by providing exposure to the variety of service organizations in their community. He invites individuals from organizations to speak in classes so that students become aware of the group's purpose and learn about available service opportunities, jobs, training experiences, leadership opportunities, and the kinds of skills that build their self-confidence and strengthen their résumés. In social studies classes, students earn points for participation in community service groups.

Offer creative events that document cultural communities

The arts provide students with opportunities to address rigorous academic standards in ways that go beyond paper-and-pencil assignments. Through photography, drawing, painting, and other media, students research and document topics of interest, typically describing their work in a formal oral presentation.

At Hoover School, Mr. Izumi organizes an annual Cultural Communities event where students in grades 3–8 present their interpretation of "their cultural community," defined as what they believe to be the greatest influence on their values and practices. They use a specific medium to do this—photography, drawing, painting, or music video. The medium changes every year, and a different artist is invited in to assist students with their work, which is linked to the social studies curriculum. Teachers also help students explore how they would like to portray their community. One interesting aspect of the project is to see the various ways diverse groups of students express their ideas of a cultural community. Older students sometimes consider their cultural community to be their peers and the music they enjoy. As a culminating event, the projects are presented formally in class. Afterward, an evening event is held where the work is displayed in the auditorium for families and the community to view. The Cultural Communities evening is a favorite event because, in addition to providing a forum for student self-reflection and self-expression, families tell Mr. Izumi that they enjoy learning about all the different students and mingling with adults from the various ethnic groups at the school.

An option for younger students is a Family Backpack Project (Schrodt, Fain, & Hasty, 2015), which involves using high-quality picture books that represent children and families from diverse backgrounds to encourage family participation in the curriculum. After four books have been read and discussed in class, each child chooses one of the books to take home, along with a response journal and letter to parents inviting them and their child to respond to the text in the journal in any way they choose: by drawing, by writing in any language, by pasting in photographs, and so on. After a week of reading and responding at home, students form literature circles with others who chose the same book and share their journals and discuss the book. To encourage ongoing family–school collaboration, the same process repeats each month with a different set of books.

● ● ●

Creating positive student–teacher relationships is at the core of reaching hard-to-teach students. In fact, it is at the core of *all* effective teaching. We have seen, time and time again, that students will perform better for those teachers who show them respect and show respect for their families, their cultures, and their home languages. Doing the intentional work necessary to create and sustain a school climate that is positive and supportive, which includes implementing the kinds of culturally responsive practices we've discussed in this chapter, is a more than worthy investment. In fact, of the five essential practices critical to reaching students who are hard to teach, it probably offers the biggest bang for the buck.

Conclusion

Reaching the hardest to teach is not a spectator sport; standing on the sidelines won't change the outcome of the game. If you are a teacher, one way to begin taking action in your own classroom is to ask yourself these reflective questions after every lesson you teach:

- Did I model the thinking and language I expected from my students?
- Were the lesson's learning target, purpose, and success criteria clear?
- Did students have sufficient opportunities to consolidate their learning with peers?
- Did I address errors and misconceptions early on, as students completed rigorous tasks?

If the answers to these questions are yes, move on to examine the systems of supports available in your classroom. Reflect on these questions:

- Do I provide access to the core curriculum through strong differentiated instruction?

- Is the learning climate I create supportive of all students as individuals, and how do I know this?
- Are my expectations appropriately and consistently high, and do I provide scaffolds when and where they are needed?
- Do students receive supplemental and intensive interventions when the data suggest they need it?
- Did all students receive the appropriate kind of language support in content lessons?
- Did students receive the appropriate kind of language instruction?
- What additional assessments could shed light on what students need to be taught?

Together, these questions and the actions that they spur provide the means to move any student who struggles toward greater success in school. Any student is teachable once you know how to approach the challenge. Given the proper attention and support, the students you find hardest to teach will reveal themselves to be the individuals they really are—geniuses in their own right, destined to contribute to the world in unique and powerful ways.

References

Abedi, J., Leon, S., & Kao, J. C. (2008). *Examining differential item functioning in reading assessments for students with disabilities* (CRESST Report No. 744). Los Angeles: University of California, National Center for Research on Evaluation, Standards, and Student Testing.

Allen, J. A., Gregory, A., Mikami, A., Lun, J., Hamre, B., & Pianta, R. (2013). Observations of effective teacher-student interactions in secondary school classrooms: Predicting student achievement with the Classroom Assessment Scoring System—secondary. *School Psychology Review, 42*(1), 76–97.

Anagnostopoulous, D. (2003). The new accountability, student failure, and teachers' work in urban high schools. *Educational Policy, 17*(3), 291–316.

Atwood, V. A., & Wilen, W. W. (1991). Wait time and effective social studies instruction: What can research in science education tell us? *Social Education, 55*(3), 179–181.

August, D., & Shanahan, D. (2010). Effective English literacy instruction for English learners. In California Department of Education (Ed.), *Improving education for English learners: Research-based approaches* (pp. 209–249). Sacramento, CA: CDE Press.

Baily, F., & Pransky, K. (2014). *Memory at work in the classroom: Strategies to help underachieving students.* Alexandria, VA: ASCD.

Beaudoin, M. N. (2011, September). Respect—Where do we start? *Educational Leadership, 69*(1), 40–44.

Berliner, D. C., & Biddle, B. J. (1996). *The manufactured crisis: Myths, fraud, and the attack on America's public schools.* New York: Basic Books.

Bondie, R., Gaughram, L., & Zusho, A. (2015, November). Fostering English learners' confidence. *Educational Leadership, 72*(3), 42–46.

Chall, J., & Jacobs, V. A. (2003, Spring). The classic study on poor children's fourth-grade slump. *American Educator, 27*(1), 14–15, 44.

Coggins, D., Kravin, D., Coates, G. D., & Carroll, M. D. (2007). *English language learners in the mathematics classroom.* Thousand Oaks, CA: Corwin.

Cruz, B. (2015, March). The problem we still live with. *Educational Leadership, 72*(6), 16–20.

Davis, A. P., & McGrail, E. (2009, March). The joy of blogging. *Educational Leadership, 66*(6), 74–77.

Davis, S., & Nixon, C. (2011, September). What students say about bullying. *Educational Leadership, 69*(1), 18–23.

Dunning, S., & Stafford, W. (1992). *Getting the knack: 20 poetry writing exercises.* Urbana, IL: National Council of Teachers of English.

Dweck, C. S. (2006). *Mindset: The new psychology of success.* New York: Ballantine Books.

Echevarría, J., & Graves, A. (2015). *Sheltered content instruction: Teaching students with diverse abilities* (5th ed.). Boston: Allyn & Bacon.

Echevarría, J., Richards-Tutor, C., Canges, R., & Francis, D. (2011). Using the SIOP® Model to promote the acquisition of language and science concepts with English learners. *Bilingual Research Journal, 34*(3), 334–351.

Echevarría, J., Richards-Tutor, C., & Vogt, M. (2015). *Response to intervention (RTI) and English learners: Using the SIOP® Model* (2nd ed.). Boston: Allyn & Bacon.

Echevarría, J., & Short, D. (2010). Programs and practices for effective sheltered content instruction. In California Department of Education (Ed.), *Improving education for English learners: Research-based approaches* (pp. 250–321). Sacramento, CA: CDE Press.

Echevarría, J., Short, D., & Vogt, M. (2008). *Implementing the SIOP® Model through effective professional development and coaching.* Boston: Allyn & Bacon.

Echevarría, J., Vogt, M. E., & Short, D. (2000). *Making content comprehensible for English learners: The SIOP® Model.* Boston: Allyn & Bacon.

Echevarría, J., Vogt, M. E., & Short, D. (2017). *Making content comprehensible for English learners: The SIOP® Model* (5th ed.). Boston: Allyn & Bacon.

Elliott, S. N. (2015). Measuring opportunity to learn and achievement growth: Key research issues with implications for the effective education of all students. *Remedial & Special Education, 36*(1), 58–64.

Espin, C. A., Shin, J., & Busch, T. W. (2005). Curriculum-based measurement in the content areas: Vocabulary matching as an indicator of progress in social studies learning. *Journal of Learning Disabilities, 38*(4), 353–363.

Ferlazzo, L. (2011, May). Involvement or engagement? *Educational Leadership, 68*(8), 10–14.

Fisher, D. (2009). The use of instructional time in the typical high school classroom. *The Educational Forum, 73,* 168–176.

Fisher, D. & Frey, N. (2007). *Scaffolded writing instruction: Teaching with a gradual-release framework.* New York: Scholastic.

Fisher, D., & Frey, N. (2010). *Enhancing RTI: How to ensure success with effective classroom instruction and intervention.* Alexandria, VA: ASCD.

Fisher, D., & Frey, N. (2011). *The purposeful classroom: How to structure lessons with learning goals in mind.* Alexandria, VA: ASCD.

Fisher, D., & Frey, N. (2013). *Better learning through structured teaching: A framework for the gradual release of responsibility* (2nd ed.). Alexandria, VA: ASCD.

Fisher, D., & Frey, N. (2014). Close reading as an intervention for struggling middle school readers. *Journal of Adolescent and Adult Literacy, 57*(5), 367–376.

Fisher, D., Frey, N., Anderson, H., & Thayre, M. (2015). *Text-dependent questions: Pathways to close and critical reading, grades K–5.* Thousand Oaks, CA: Corwin.

Fisher, D., Frey, N., & Arzonetti Hite, S. (2016). *Intentional and targeted teaching: A framework for teacher growth and leadership.* Alexandria, VA: ASCD.

Fisher, D., Frey, N., & Rothenberg, C. (2008). *Content area conversations: How to plan discussion-based lessons for diverse language learners.* Alexandria, VA: ASCD.

Frey, N., Fisher, D., & Nelson, J. (2013). It's all about the talk. *Kappan, 94*(6), 8–13.

Frey, N., Lapp, D., & Fisher, D. (2009). The academic booster shot: In-school tutoring to prevent grade-level retention. In J. Richards & C. Lassonde (Eds.), *Literacy tutoring that works: A look at successful in-school, after-school, and summer programs* (pp. 32–45). Newark, DE: International Reading Association.

Gay, G. (2010). *Culturally responsive teaching: Theory, research, and practice* (2nd ed.). New York: Teachers College Press.

Ginsburg, A., Jordan, P., & Chang, H. (2014). *Absences add up: How school attendance influences school success.* Retrieved from http://www.attendanceworks.org/wordpress/wp-content/uploads/2014/09/Absenses-Add-Up_090114-1-1.pdf

Giroir, S., Grimaldo, L., Vaughn, S., & Roberts, G. (2015). Interactive read-alouds for English learners in the elementary grades. *Reading Teacher, 68*(8), 639–648.

Goldenberg, C. (2013). Unlocking the research on English learners: What we know—and don't yet know—about effective instruction. *American Educator, 37*(2), 4–11, 38.

Guthrie, J. T., & Wigfield, A. (2000). Engagement and motivation in reading. In M. L. Kamil, P. B. Mosenthal, P. D. Pearson, & R. Barr (Eds.), *Handbook of reading research* (Vol. III, pp. 403–424). Mahwah, NJ: Erlbaum.

Hattie, J. (2009). *Visible learning: A synthesis of over 800 meta-analyses relating to achievement.* New York: Routledge.

Hernandez, F., & Kose, B. W. (2012). The developmental model of intercultural sensitivity: A tool for understanding principals' cultural competence. *Education & Urban Society, 44*(4), 512–530.

Huddleston, A. (2014). Achievement at whose expense? A literature review of test-based grade retention policies in U.S. schools. *Education Policy Analysis Archives, 22*(18), 1–31.

Jackson, K. F. (2009). Building cultural competence: A systematic evaluation of the effectiveness of culturally sensitive interventions with ethnic minority youth. *Children & Youth Services Review, 31*(11), 1192–1198.

Jasmine, J., & Schiesl, P. (2009). The effects of word walls and word wall activities on the reading fluency of first grade students. *Reading Horizons, 49*(4), 301–314.

Kafele, B. (2013). *Closing the attitude gap: How to fire up your students to strive for success.* Alexandria, VA: ASCD.

Kagan, S. (1994). *Cooperative learning.* San Clemente, CA: Kagan Publishing.

Kaufman, J. S., Jaser, S. S., Vaughan, E. L., Reynolds, J. S., Di Donato, J., Bernard, S. N., & Hernandez-Brereton, M. (2010). Patterns in office referral data by grade, race/ethnicity, and gender. *Journal of Positive Behavior Interventions, 12*(1), 44–54.

Kena, G., Aud, S., Johnson, F., Wang, X., Zhang, J., Rathbun, A., Wilkinson-Flicker, S., & Kristapovich, P. (2014). *The condition of education 2014* (NCES 2014-083). Washington, DC: U.S. Department of Education, National Center for Education Statistics. Retrieved from http://nces.ed.gov/pubs2014/2014083.pdf

Kidd, J. M. (2011). Unlearning color blindness and learning from families. In P. R. Schmidt & A. M. Lazar (Eds.), *Practicing what we teach* (pp. 218–234). New York: Teachers College Press.

Kraft, M. A., & Rogers, T. (2015). The underutilized potential of teacher-to-parent communication: Evidence from a field experiment. *Economics of Education Review, 47*(2015), 49–63.

Layne, S. (2015). *In defense of read-aloud: Sustaining best practice.* Portland, ME: Stenhouse.

LeDoux, J. (1996). *The emotional brain.* New York: Simon & Schuster.

Lindsey, R. B., Nuri Robins, K. J., & Terrell, R. D. (2009). *Cultural proficiency: A manual for school leadership* (3rd ed.). Thousand Oaks, CA: Corwin.

Lindsey, R. B., Roberts, L. M., & Campbell Jones, F. (2013). *The culturally proficient school: An implementation guide for school leaders* (2nd ed.). Thousand Oaks, CA: Corwin.

Marzano, R. J., Marzano, J. S., & Pickering, D. J. (2003). *Classroom management that works: Research-based strategies for every teacher.* Alexandria, VA: ASCD.

Miller, A. K. (2015). *Freedom to fail: How do I foster risk-taking and innovation in my classroom?* (ASCD Arias). Alexandria, VA: ASCD.

Ross, S. M., McDonald, A. J., Alberg, M., & McSparrin-Gallagher, B. (2007). Achievement and climate outcomes for the Knowledge Is Power Program in an inner-city middle school. *Journal of Education for Students Placed at Risk, 12*(2), 137–165.

Rowe, M. B. (1987, Spring). Wait time: Slowing down may be a way of speeding up. *American Educator, 11,* 38–43, 47.

Samuels, C. A. (2014). Read-aloud option boosts NAEP achievement, study finds. *Education Week, 33*(26), 15.

Santoro, N., & Allard, A. (2005). (Re)examining identities: Working with diversity in the pre-service teaching experience. *Teaching and Teacher Education, 21*(7), 863–873.

Saunders, W. M., & Goldenberg, C. (2010). Research to guide English language development instruction. In D. Dolson & L. Burnham-Massey (Eds.), *Improving education for English learners: Research-based approaches.* Sacramento, CA: CDE Press.

Saunders, W., Goldenberg, C., & Marcelletti, D. (2013, Summer). English language development: Guidelines for instruction. *American Educator, 37*(2), 13–25, 38–39.

Schmidt, W. H., Burroughs, N. A., Zoido, P., & Houang, R. T. (2015). The role of schooling in perpetuating educational inequality: An international perspective. *Educational Researcher, 44,* 371–386.

Schrodt, K., Fain, J. G., & Hasty, M. (2015). Exploring culturally relevant texts with kindergartners and their families. *The Reading Teacher,* 68(8), 589–598.

Short, D., & Echevarría, J. (2016). *Developing academic language using the SIOP® Model.* Boston: Allyn & Bacon.

Short, D., Echevarría, J., & Richards-Tutor, C. (2011). Research on academic literacy development in sheltered instruction classrooms. *Language Teaching Research, 15*(3), 363–380.

Short, D. J., & Fitzsimmons, S. (2007). *Double the work: Challenges and solutions to acquiring language and academic literacy for adolescent English language learners. A report to Carnegie Corporation of New York.* Washington, DC: Alliance for Excellent Education.

Smit, R., & Humpert, W. (2012). Differentiated instruction in small schools. *Teaching & Teacher Education, 28*(8), 1152–1162.

Smith, D., Fisher, D., & Frey, N. (2015). *Better than carrots or sticks: Restorative practices for positive classroom management.* Alexandria, VA: ASCD.

Snyder, T. D., & Dillow, S. A. (2015). *Digest of Education Statistics 2013* (NCES 2015-011). Washington, DC: U.S. Department of Education, National Center for Education Statistics, Institute of Education Sciences.

Stahl, K. (2012). Complex text or frustration-level text: Using shared reading to bridge the difference. *The Reading Teacher, 66*(1), 47–51.

Steinmayr, R., & Spinath, B. (2009). The importance of motivation as a predictor of student achievement. *Learning and Individual Differences, 19*(1), 80–90.

Taba, H. (1967). *Teachers' handbook to elementary social studies.* Reading, MA: Addison-Wesley.

Taylor, W. L. (1953). Cloze procedure: A new tool for measuring readability. *Journalism Quarterly, 30,* 415–433.

Tobin, T., & Sugai, G. (1999). Using sixth grade school records to predict violence, chronic discipline problems, and high school outcomes. *Journal of Emotional and Behavioral Disorders, 7*(1), 40–53.

Tomlinson, C. A. (2001). *How to differentiate instruction in mixed-ability classrooms* (2nd ed.). Alexandria, VA: ASCD.

Villa, R., Thousand, J., & Nevin, A. (2013). *A guide to co-teaching: New lessons and strategies to facilitate student learning* (3rd ed.). Thousand Oaks, CA: Corwin.

Vogt, M. E., & Echevarría, J. (2008). *99 ideas and activities for teaching English learners with the SIOP® Model.* Boston: Allyn & Bacon.

Vogt, M. E., Echevarría, J., & Washam, M. (2015). *99 MORE ideas and activities for teaching English learners with the SIOP® Model.* Boston: Allyn & Bacon.

Wilkinson, I. A. G., & Nelson, K. (2013). Role of discussion in reading comprehension. In J. Hattie & E. M. Anderson (Eds.), *International guide to student achievement* (pp. 299–302). New York: Routledge.

Winograd, P., & Paris, S. G. (1989). A cognitive and motivational agenda for reading instruction. *Educational Leadership, 46*(4), 30–36.

Wolf, M. (2008). *Proust and the squid: The story and science of the reading brain.* New York: Harper.

Wright, J. A., & Dusek, J. B. (1998). Compiling school base rates for disruptive behaviors from student referral data. *School Psychology Review, 27*(1), 138–148.

Zau, A. C., & Betts, J. R. (2008). *Predicting success, preventing failure: An investigation of the California High School Exit Exam.* Sacramento: Public Policy Institute of California.

Zwiers, J., & Crawford, M. (2011). *Academic conversations: Classroom talk that fosters critical thinking and content understandings.* Portland, ME: Stenhouse.

Index

Note: Page references followed by an *f* indicate information contained in figures.

absenteeism, chronic, 8
academic language instruction, 32–33,
    106–108, 107*f*, 114, 126–129
academic risk taking, 23
academic vocabulary use. *See*
    academic language instruction
access to the core curriculum
    about, 9, 14, 38–40
    accommodations and
        modifications, 64–67
    cognitive and linguistic modeling,
        41–42
    collaborative learning, 42
    differentiated content, 45–50
    differentiated instruction, 42–64,
        44*f*–45*f*, 58*f*
    differentiated learning processes,
        50–57, 58*f*
    differentiated products, 57–64
    expectations and relevance, 41
    focus on high-quality instruction,
        40–42
accommodations, 64–66, 73–74, 74*f*
admit slips, 83–85
advisory periods, daily, 63
allocation of instructional time, 14, 25,
    26, 70–72
Alpha Writer Deluxe (software), 87
Amante, Ivan, 62–63

Aquino, Rafael, 103–106
aspirations, fostering student, 18–19,
    34–37
assessment-informed instruction
    about, 11, 68–70
    accommodations and validity in,
        73–74, 74*f*
    and allocation of instructional
        resources, 14, 26, 70–72
    assessment principles, 72–76,
        74*f*, 76*f*
    data-based intervention design,
        96–102
    and English learners, 75–76,
        108–110, 109*f*, 128–129
    frequency of assessment, 72–73
    language learning assessment,
        73
    language profiles and, 108–110,
        109*f*
    needs-based instruction, 75
    projects and portfolios for
        assessment, 88–92
    RTI^2 (response to instruction and
        intervention), 96–102
    speaking and listening
        assessments, 76–82
    specialists' consultation on,
        75–76

assessment-informed instruction
(continued)
    student involvement and goal
        setting, 92–96, 93f, 95f
    writing assessments, 82–88, 84f
assistive technology, 39
Aurasma app, 78

Barrier Games, 123f
blogs, personal, 86–87
"Blue Eyes/Brown Eyes" exercise
    (Elliott), 37
Brooks, Crystal, 27
Browning, Darnell, 31–34
Bryant, Demetrius, 81–82
bullying, 153–154
Busy Bees, 123f

career planning, 34–37
Carlson, Daniel, 46
Casey, Frank, 113–114
Cervantes, Lisa, 79–80
Chai, Bao, 152–153
checking for understanding. See also
    assessment-informed instruction
    about, 27
    digital tools for, 77–80
    group checks, 80–82
    projects and portfolios for, 88–92
    speaking and listening
        assessments, 76–82
    writing assessments, 82–88, 84f
choice, product, 59–62
Cisse, Joseph, 48
classroom learning environments
    about, 9–10, 134–137
    assessing culture and climate,
        141–146
    bullying, 153–154
    climate defined, 135–136
    colorblindness, 152–153
    cultural community
        documentation, 156–157
    cultural competence, 138–141
    cultural sensitivity, 140–141
    culture defined, 135
    families and home life of
        students, 142–146
    honoring student experiences,
        147–148
    institutionalizing cultural
        knowledge, 154–157

classroom learning environments
(continued)
    language of respect, 148–150, 149f
    managing differences, 150–154
    opportunities to expand
        students' experiences, 155–156
    positive conflict, 150–152
    positive student-teacher
        relationships, 14, 137–138
    showing care and concern,
        146–147
    teacher cultural self-awareness,
        141
    teachers' current beliefs and
        biases, 142–143
    value in diversity, 146–150, 149f
climate, school, 135–136. See also
    classroom learning environments
cognates, discipline-specific, 114.
    See also vocabulary, academic and
    discipline-specific
cognitive and linguistic modeling,
    41–42, 52–53
collaborative conversations, 126–127
Collaborative Dialogue, 123f
collaborative learning, 12, 40, 42
Collaborative Poster, 121–122
college-going culture, 37
colorblindness, 152–153
conferences, with students, 92–94,
    93f
conferencing form, 93f
content accommodations, 65
content differentiation, 43, 44f–45f,
    45–50
content instruction, language
    instruction and, 112–115
content modifications, 66
content-specific word walls, 114–115
Conversational Roundtable, 120–121,
    121f
critical thinking skills, 110–111
Cruz, Olivia, 118
Cuéllar, Mario, 18–21
Cultivating a Learning Climate, 12
cultural community documentation,
    156–157
cultural competence, 138–141
The Culturally Proficient School
    (Lindsey, Roberts, and Jones), 141
cultural proficiency, 139–140
cultural sensitivity, 140–141

culture, school, 135. *See also*
    classroom learning environments
curricular access. *See* access to the
    core curriculum

D'Angelo, Janelle, 98–99
Daniels, Omar, 110–111, 127–128
decision tasks, differentiating, 46–47
differentiated instruction
    about, 9, 42–44
    content, 43, 44f–45f, 45–50
    learning processes, 44, 44f–45f,
        50–57, 58f
    products, 44, 44f–45f, 57–64
digital portfolios, 18–19, 89–90
digital student folders, 86
digital tools for assessment, 77–80
digital writing prompts, 83–85
disabilities, students with. *See* special
    education
discipline-specific academic language,
    107f, 114. *See also* academic
    language instruction; English
    language instruction
diversity, value in, 141, 146–150, 149f
dropping out of school, 22
Duong, Tina, 63

Edmodo system, 86
effort and results links, 23
El-Amin, Zara, 90
Elbow Partner Exchange, 119–120
Elliott, Jane, 37
Elwardi, Rita, 1–5
Emeka, Tanya, 88–89
emotional support, 137–138
English language instruction
    about, 103–106
    academic language, 32–33,
        106–108, 107f, 126–129
    assessment-informed instruction,
        75–76, 128–129
    basic group work routines, 116–118
    cognates, 114
    collaborative conversations,
        126–127
    Collaborative Poster, 121–122
    content-specific word walls,
        114–115
    Conversational Roundtable,
        120–121, 121f
    critical thinking skills and,
        110–111

English language instruction
    (continued)
    digital tools to assist, 78
    Elbow Partner Exchange, 119–120
    experiences and knowledge of
        students, 111
    explicit language instruction
        classes (ELD/ESL), 129–133
    foundational literacy skills, 110
    grade-level expectations and,
        30–31
    Homework Rounds, 120
    importance of, 10–11, 14
    integration into content
        instruction, 112–115
    Jigsaw, 122–123
    language frames, 112–114
    language profiles and
        assessment, 108–110, 109f
    learning intentions for, 32–34
    Novel Ideas Only, 117–118
    and opportunity to learn, 24–25
    outmoded methods, 7
    peer collaboration and, 115–123,
        121f, 122f, 124f, 125f
    productive group work routines,
        118–123, 121f, 122f, 124f, 125f
    scaffolded instruction, 127–128
    Think-Pair-Square, 117
    Turn to Your Partner and—
        prompt, 117
    visual supports, 128
    wait time and, 29
Evans, Jeffrey, 122
excellent instruction, 9–12, 14–17
exit cards, 68–69, 85
expectations for success
    about, 10, 13, 14
    clear learning intentions,
        29–34
    clear success criteria, 29–31
    example scenario, 18–21
    fostering student aspirations,
        34–37
    goal setting, 29–31
    grade-level expectations, 30
    lesson pace, 25–27
    maximizing lesson time, 27
    presuming success, 21–23
    teaching with urgency, 23–29
    using wait time, 28–29
Explorers and Settlers, 124f
Expressive Builder (software), 79–80

families, of students, 100, 142–146
Family Backpack Project, 157
Find Someone Who . . ., 124f
FIT Teaching (Framework for Intentional and Targeted Teaching), 11, 12, 41
Flipagram (app), 90
focused instruction, 12
formative assessment, 43
foundational skills gaps, 110
found poems, 3–4, 85
Found Poetry, 3–4
frames, language, 112–114
Framework for Intentional and Targeted Teaching (FIT Teaching), 11, 12, 41
frontloading information, 55
fuzzy tasks, differentiating, 48–50

Garcia, Arleta, 110
Garcia, Ryan, 142–143, 144–145
generative sentences, 82–83, 84f
Genius Hour, 62, 63–64
Glogster (website), 89
goal setting, 29–31, 92–96, 93f, 95f
Gomez, Alicia, 14–17
GoSoapBox app, 81–82
grade-level expectations, 30
grade point averages, 22
group work routines. See peer collaboration routines
growth mindset, 23
"guess what's in the teacher's head" questions, 77
guided instruction, 12, 53–54
guided practice, 42

Haiku system, 86
Harden, Jennifer, 150–152
hardest-to-teach children, 6–8
Hernandez, Sarita, 90
Hightower, April, 129
Hogan, Audrey, 150–152
home visits, 144–145
Homework Rounds, 120
Hoover School, 154–157
Humphrey, Frank, 98

inclusion support specialists, 75
inclusive educational practices, 22
independent learning, 12
independent studies, 62
Ingersol, Matt, 121

Inside/Outside Circles, 124f
instruction
    access to (See access to the core curriculum)
    assessment and (See assessment-informed instruction)
    data-based intervention design, 96–102
    differentiated content, 45–50
    differentiated instruction, 42–44, 44f–45f
    differentiated learning processes, 50–57, 58f
    differentiated products, 57–64
    excellent instruction, 9–12, 14–17
    focused instruction, 12
    focus on high-quality, 40–42
    guided instruction, 12
    instructional resource allocation, 14, 25, 26, 70–72
    instructional time allocation, 14, 26
    Instruction with Intention, 12
    pace of lessons, 25–27
instructions, visual and verbal, 26–27
internships, 37
Izumi, Phillip, 154–157

Jigsaw, 122–123
judgment tasks, differentiating, 47

Kidblog, 86
kidzsearch, 46

language frames, 112–114
language function, 32
language instruction. See English language instruction
language of respect, 148–150, 149f
language profiles and assessment, 108–110, 109f
language structure, 32
learned helplessness, 23
learning environments. See classroom learning environments
learning intentions, 29–34, 40, 41
learning journeys, 18
learning processes
    accommodations for, 65
    differentiation of, 44, 44f–45f, 50–57, 58f
    modifications of, 66
learning stations, 77–78

lesson pace, 25–27
lesson planning, relevance and, 41
lesson time, maximizing, 24, 27
letters, 85
leveled questions, 54–57, 58*f*
Liang, Jeremy, 86–87
library use, 64
Lindbergh School, 134–135, 140–141
linguistic modeling, 41–42
listening and speaking assessments,
    76–82
listening instruction, specialized,
    131–132
Lopez, Dalia, 80–81

magical thinking, 20
McDonald, Judith, 146–148
mentors, 37
metacognition, 49, 82
Miller, Andrea, 122–123
"minute math," 27
modeling, cognitive and linguistic, 40,
    41–42, 52–53
modifications to instruction, 66–67
Monroe, Kendra, 131
Montessori education, 87
Montrose, Kenya, 47, 49
motivation, student, 59–60
MTSS (Multi-Tiered Systems of
    Support), 96
Multi-Tiered Systems of Support
    (MTSS), 96

Niño, Lina, 131–132
Novel Ideas Only, 117–118
Numbered Heads Together, 124*f*

"one and done" reading model, 55, 56
Ononiwu, Alice, 39
open-ended projects, 62–64
Opinion Stations, 118
opportunity to learn (OTL), 13–14,
    24–25

pace of lessons, 25–27
parents. *See* families, of students
Parsons, Ken, 108–110
Pavri, Aalya, 119
peer collaboration routines
    about, 115–116
    Barrier Games, 123*f*
    Busy Bees, 123*f*

peer collaboration routines
    (continued)
        collaborative conversations,
            126–127
        Collaborative Dialogue, 123*f*
        Collaborative Poster, 121–122
        Conversational Roundtable,
            120–121, 121*f*
        Elbow Partner Exchange, 119–120
        Explorers and Settlers, 124*f*
        Find Someone Who . . , 124*f*
        Homework Rounds, 120
        Inside/Outside Circles, 124*f*
        Jigsaw, 122–123
        Novel Ideas Only, 117–118
        Numbered Heads Together,
            124*f*
        Opinion Stations, 118
        Reciprocal Teaching, 125*f*
        Study Buddy Teaming, 125*f*
        Think-Pair-Square, 117
        Think-Write-Pair-Share, 125*f*
        Three Step Interviews, 125*f*
        Turn to Your Partner and—
            prompt, 117
        Walking Review, 124*f*
portfolios for assessment, 89–92
positive conflict, 150–152
positive student-teacher
    relationships, 14, 137–138
positive thinking, 20
problem-based learning, 48–49
problem tasks, differentiating, 47–48
process. *See* learning process
product accommodations, 65
product differentiation, 44, 44*f*–45*f*,
    57–64
product modifications, 66
projects and portfolios for
    assessment, 88–92

questioning students, 28–29, 54–57,
    58*f*, 77
quick-writes, 1–3, 3*f*, 27
Quinn, Mark, 47

Rahal, Noura, 56–57
read-alouds, 50–51
reading comprehension, 50
reading instruction, specialized,
    130–131
Reciprocal Teaching, 125*f*

relationships with struggling students, 14, 137–138

relevance of curricula, 41

resource allocation, instructional, 14, 25, 26, 70–72

response to instruction and intervention (RTI²). *See* RTI² (response to instruction and intervention)

restorative practices, 153

retention, 22

Richards, Kendra, 79

Rodriguez, Emma, 71–72

Roosevelt School, 103–106

Rowe, Mary Budd, 28

RTI² (response to instruction and intervention)
    implementation examples, 98–99
    levels of, 96–97
    misconceptions, 97–98
    results, 99–100
    schoolwide practices, 100–102

Sanchez, Maria, 54

sarcasm, 148

scaffolded learning
    about, 9, 14, 40
    and English language instruction, 112–114, 127–128
    guided instruction, 53–54
    leveled questions, 54–57
    modeling as, 41–42

school climate and culture. *See* classroom learning environments

script outlines with prompts, 49

Seesaw digital portfolio (app), 89–90

self-assessment form, 95f

Sheldon, Jeff, 54

Sheltered Instructional Observation Protocol (SIOP)
    about, 11, 12
    differentiation and, 43
    language objectives in, 112

Socrative system (app), 80

speaking and listening assessments, 76–82

speaking instruction, specialized, 131–132

special education
    about, 6
    accommodations and modifications, 64–67

special education (continued)
    home visits and, 144
    and opportunity to learn, 24–25
    remedial classes and, 40

Spencer, Haley, 27

stereotypes, cultural, 142–143

students. *See also* peer collaboration routines
    collaborative learning, 42
    experiences and knowledge of, 111, 155–156
    families and home life, 142–146
    involvement and goal setting, 92–96, 93f, 95f
    involvement in planning learning, 94–96, 95f
    language profiles of, 108–110, 109f
    positive relationships with teachers, 14, 137–138

Study Buddy Teaming, 125f

success, expectations for. *See* expectations for success

success criteria, communicating, 29–31, 41

summative assessment feedback, 86

Swanson, Maxwell, 117

Sweet Search 4 Me (website), 88–89

tablets, 78

take a stand, 85

teachers
    beliefs and biases of, 142–143
    cultural self-awareness, 141
    honoring student experiences, 147–148
    impact on student achievement, 136
    language of respect, 148–150, 149f
    positive relationships with students, 14, 137–138
    showing care and concern, 146–147
    and student home life, 142–146

technology for assessment, 77–80

TED Talks, 128

Tell About This app, 79

think-alouds, 51–53

Think-Pair-Square, 117

Think-Write-Pair-Share, 125f

Three Step Interviews, 3, 125f

timers, using in classroom, 26

transitions, 26
Turn to Your Partner and— prompt,
    117

Universal Design for Learning (UDL)
    digital book, 47
Uribe, Alex, 68–69

visual supports, for language learners,
    128
vocabulary, academic and discipline-
    specific, 32–33, 106–108, 107*f*, 114,
    126–129

wait time, 28–29
Walking Review, 124*f*
Washington, Laurie, 87–88
Weinberg, Brad, 77–78
whole-class questioning, 77
word walls, content-specific, 114–115
writing assessments, 82–88, 84*f*
writing instruction, specialized,
    130–131

YouTube, 128

About the Authors

 **Jana Echevarría** is a professor emerita at California State University, Long Beach, where she was selected as Outstanding Professor in 2005. She has taught elementary and secondary students in general education, special education, ESL, and bilingual programs. A founding researcher of the SIOP Model, Jana focuses on effective instruction for English learners, including those with learning disabilities. Her publications include more than 60 books, book chapters, and journal articles. She has presented her research in the United States and internationally, including at Oxford University (England), Wits University (South Africa), Harvard University (United States), Stanford University (United States), University of Barcelona (Spain), and South East Europe University (Macedonia), where she was a Fulbright Specialist. Currently, Jana serves as the ELL expert for the U.S. Department of Justice on the *Lau v. SFUSD* case. She can be reached through her blog site, www.janaechevarria.com.

Nancy Frey is a professor of educational leadership at San Diego State University and a teacher leader at Health Sciences High & Middle College. Nancy is a recipient of the Christa McAuliffe Award for Excellence in Teacher Education from the American Association of State Colleges and Universities and the Early Career Award from the Literacy Research Association. She has published many articles and books on literacy and instruction, including *Productive Group Work: How to Engage Students, Build Teamwork, and Promote Understanding; The Formative Assessment Action Plan: Practical Steps to More Successful Teaching and Learning;* and *Guided Instruction: How to Develop Confident and Successful Learners.* She can be reached at nfrey@mail.sdsu.edu.

Douglas Fisher is a professor of educational leadership at San Diego State University and a teacher leader at Health Sciences High & Middle College. He is a member of the California Reading Hall of Fame and was honored as an exemplary leader by the Conference on English Leadership. He has published numerous articles on improving student achievement, and his books include *The Purposeful Classroom: How to Structure Lessons with Learning Goals in Mind; Enhancing RTI: How to Ensure Success with Effective Classroom Instruction and Intervention; Checking for Understanding: Formative Assessment Techniques for Your Classroom; How to Create a Culture of Achievement in Your School and Classroom;* and *Intentional and Targeted Teaching: A Framework for Teacher Growth and Leadership.* He can be reached at dfisher@mail.sdsu.edu.

Related ASCD Resources: Effective Instruction for Struggling Students

At the time of publication, the following ASCD resources were available (ASCD stock numbers appear in parentheses). For up-to-date information about ASCD resources, go to www.ascd.org. You can search the complete archives of *Educational Leadership* at www.ascd.org/el.

ASCD Edge Group
Exchange ideas and connect with other educators on the social networking site ASCD EDge® at http://ascdedge.ascd.org

Online Courses
Literacy Strategies: Improving Comprehension (mobile-friendly) (#PD09OC51M)
Teaching with Poverty in Mind (#PD11OC139M)

Print Products
Educational Leadership: Reaching the Reluctant Learner (#108025)
Enhancing RTI: How to Ensure Success with Effective Classroom Instruction and Intervention by Douglas Fisher and Nancy Frey (#110037)
Getting to "Got It!" Helping Struggling Students Learn How to Learn by Betty K. Garner (#107024)
Hanging In: Strategies for Teaching the Students Who Challenge Us Most by Jeffrey Benson (#144013)
How to Support Struggling Students (Mastering the Principles of Great Teaching series) by Robyn R. Jackson and Claire Lambert (#110073)
Learning to Choose, Choosing to Learn: The Key to Student Motivation and Achievement by Mike Anderson (#116015)
Unlocking Student Potential: How do I identify and activate student strengths? (ASCD Arias) by Yvette Jackson and Veronica A. McDermott (#SF115057)

Video
Breaking Through Barriers to Achievement (DVD and Facilitator's Guide) (#605133)
Educating Everybody's Children (DVD) (#600228)

For more information: send e-mail to member@ascd.org; call 1-800-933-2723 or 703-578-9600, press 2; send a fax to 703-575-5400; or write to Information Services, ASCD, 1703 N. Beauregard St., Alexandria, VA 22311-1714 USA.

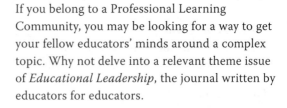